KU-567-227

LINDA ANDERSON

# TO STAY ALIVE

Futura

A Futura Book

ISBN 0 7088 2775 6

Printed and bound in Great Britain by
Hunt Barnard Printing Ltd, Aylesbury, Bucks.

Futura Publications
A Division of
Macdonald & Co (Publishers) Ltd
Maxwell House
74 Worship Street
London EC2A 2EN

A BPCC plc Company

I would like to thank my friends who encouraged me throughout the writing of this book, especially Bernard Miller, who read the work in progress with sympathy and vision.


We would like to thank Tim Pat Coogan for permission to quote from *On The Blanket* (Ward River Press), The Dolmen Press for a quotation from 'Butcher's Dozen' by Thomas Kinsella and Michael Yeats and Macmillan London Limited for quotations from 'Never Give All the Heart' and 'Under Ben Bulben', by W. B. Yeats.

*To my mother and father*

Lily. Dan looked at the blonde coat stiffened with blood. He hadn't believed Rosaleen when she rushed in distraught saying Lily was dead. Lying on the wasteground. He ran there at once, sure it was a mistake, not Lily at all . . .

Who had done this? Who had killed . . .?

For fun? Malice? Against him? Against Rosaleen?

Out of sheer bloody jealousy that they owned such a superb dog?

He kneeled down. Lily's dead brown eyes made him cry. He knew then that it was for target practice. The savage had been perfecting his aim. God, he would smother . . . Anger stopped his tears. Now what? He couldn't, mustn't have Rosaleen walking past this sight again. The dog was heavy. He felt the spine. Broken. The body would disintegrate if . . . Unless it was lifted very carefully. A rubber sheet . . . He would get one from the ward. Borrow a van. Where would he bury .   .? Think about it later. He must get her away and then he would feel whatever he had to feel . . .

Rosaleen. It was too cruel. She could not take another setback . . . Death. Nothing but death. The whole fucking city. A necropolis. 'It's my fault,' he thought, remembering all the times he had called Lily a nuisance, shoved her outside. Outside into these streets where everything, animate, inanimate, everything was requisitioned for the bloody Cause!

Anger made him move fast as he went to get sheeting, borrowed a van from a colleague without saying what for. When he got back to the wasteground, the dog was gone. He stood blinking. It was scary. Was somebody playing a joke? There was nothing to do but go home.

'Someone has moved Lily,' he said apologetically to Rosaleen. He had to repeat it.

'Oh. It must have been the army. There was a soldier looking at her this morning.'

7

'Bastards,' he said. 'Let the dead bury the dead . . . Sorry.'

He had started her crying. His own tears were pure fury. He hated the murderer, he hated the soldiers who had taken the dog. He wanted to take responsibility, carry her off somewhere for burial. It would have made him believe in her death.

He had to get a grip on himself. He was scared for Rosaleen. She was still so grieved over Aidan. The past few months could hardly have been worse.

He had not meant to mistreat the dog.

The house was in a tumult for weeks after the birth. The baby's torrential crying overlapped with their listless quarrels. Rosaleen was stoical, doing everything that had to be done. Lily became fretful and maladjusted. The baby had usurped her rightful place in the hierarchy. She even forgot her housetraining in a miscalculated bid for love. It drove Dan wild. The house was like a compost factory with its heaps of soiled nappies and Lily's 'accidents'. Dan was anxious to keep the dog away from Louis in case she decided to bestow any germ-laden licks. He kept throwing her out of the house. At first she kept vigil at the door, so that every time he glanced out he would meet her reproachful sorrowing stare. At last she discovered some kind of migratory instinct and began to disappear for long periods on little forays into the streets.

In the middle of this time of domestic chaos, Aidan was killed. Despatched to heaven. Where he awaits our prayers. Or so the priests assured them. Rosaleen was stupefied with grief. Her milk became scant. Dan had to set up the Milton and the feeds every day because she simply could not cope. Now she was still taking tranks and sleepers which Dan abhorred. He was a final year medical student with enough knowledge of side effects and addiction to make him wary of mood changing drugs. But there was more to it than that. He was wounded by her reliance on chemical solaces. It was like some subtle attack on him. Wasn't his love enough? Wasn't he there?

That very morning they had fought over Aidan. She was obsessed by the horror Aidan had felt, the loneliness. Dan told her his death must have been rapid for him, that it was her own agony, her own reconstruction of his death that was prolonged.

'You don't know what it was like for him. Time might stretch when it comes to dying.'

8

'I've seen people die.'

'Only in hospital beds! Anyway, it doesn't make you an authority!'

That was the trouble. If he tried to comfort her, she was always ready to accuse him of not caring or even of having disliked Aidan. Dan didn't tell her that he thought Aidan, in life and in death, played too big a part in their marriage.

When he first found lodgings in the area and met Rosaleen and Aidan, he assumed she was Aidan's girl. But no, he had a shifting harem of girls upon whom he inflicted his poems and sexual experiments. Rosaleen was not in that category. Dan was still jealous, imagining they enjoyed some intense spiritual ardour. They had been friends since childhood.

He liked to remember the day he started with Rosaleen. Sitting in a pub, minus Aidan for once.

'Where's Aidan?' she asked.

'Dashed off to a film. You know him. Not to have seen something amounts to an obligation to see it at once.'

'I think he has some new girlfriend,' she said.

'Don't you mind?'

'No. He's a friend, not a phallus.'

'You surprise me. He thinks sticking his prick in someone is the highest tribute.'

'He told me it was the quickest cure! But I think he's really hooked this time, whoever she is.'

Dan cupped her cheek with his good hand, and said in an accurate mimicry of Aidan's voice, 'Oh how it hurts me, loving myself so much as I do, to love you even for a single moment . . .'

'Don't! Why do you dislike him so much?'

'Because you're mad about him. He gets everything.'

She threw him a sad look. 'I've got to go. I have so much homework to do.'

'You're always talking about work. I can't figure out when you do it.'

'Yes, that's the problem.'

'Why do you want to go to university? What will you do afterwards?'

'No idea. Work, I suppose.'

'*Arbeit macht frei?*'

She looked at him avidly, as if she needed to fix and simplify him. 'You wouldn't be stealing anything from him, you know.'

9

His damaged hand was resting on the table. He moved it in a sudden selfconscious gesture.

'What happened to your hand?'

'Burnt. An accident. Years ago.'

She snatched the hand and pressed her lips to the pleated scars. With a half-whimper, he buried his face in her black wavy hair. They remained so for a few moments, until he realized what a silly sacramental pose it must seem to the people around them. He retrieved his hand.

They began to meet alone after that, although he still suspected her for a while of preferring Aidan.

He loved to hear about Rosaleen's family battles. How could he explain to her how exotic that great obligatory fusion of family life seemed to him? He told her of his own childhood seclusion in the large still house with his sad, indifferent mother. How his father had walked out, leaving only his silence in every room. The way his mother looked at him as if she were not seeing him, but remembering him. About the time he watched her inspecting her face in the mirror. She smoothed her eyebrows, drew on lipstick, eyeshadow. Her face seemed to take on a look of subtle malevolence. As if she were saying: 'I am not really here.' She lifted scissors and lopped off a few curls of her hair. The fallen strands of hair she scooped up into an envelope which she sealed and placed in a drawer. That was the moment when Dan decided not to care. He had to discipline himself into not caring, but it became simply customary, and by the time she died he was able to lean over her body, inhaling her smell of decayed olives without disgust, and plant a decorous kiss on her face without any emotion at all. By listening to Rosaleen's tirades against her family, Dan thought he was gathering clues to what kind of man she wanted.

He did not press her to make love. He would observe all the holy conventions of courtship. It was she who precipitated them into being lovers. That night when she fled from some domestic fray and arrived in his rooms weeping and furious. He thought only to comfort her. It was she who began to touch him deliberately and without haste, she who removed her clothes efficiently like an accustomed lover.

The first of many occasions. Culminating in Louis.

Her father and brother Leo went wild with rage when Rosaleen announced her pregnancy. Katrina was superior about it and offered

10

ill-timed prophylactic advice. Only the mother remained dignified. 'I've had twelve pregnancies, ten of which have come to fruition. You can marry Daniel Keenan, if he's the one for you, but mind, you don't have to. One more infant won't make a deal of difference to this house.'

Dan had to lie low for days while her father roamed from pub to pub declaring his intention to relieve Dan of his delinquent manhood for good. 'We shall marry,' he told Rosaleen.

'No.'

'Yes. I'll go and ask him.'

'Ask him! What about me?'

'Will you marry me?'

'No. You're only asking because of the baby.'

'You're only refusing because of the baby.'

While the stalemate was still unresolved, Dan did go to ask for Rosaleen's hand. The father was mollified at once and forgave him his premature samplings of the rest of her.

'I was a holy terror myself at your age. Scourge of the district.'

The whole family welcomed Dan. He was both a good catch and a poor orphan boy, irresistible object of glamour and pity. He won their consent before he obtained Rosaleen's. With his mother's legacy, he bought an abandoned house for a knockdown price, saving it from a knockdown fate. Having purchased it, he invited his new ally, Rosaleen's father, to look over it with him. Only then did he realize what a slum it was. He was ashamed, wanted to get his money back. But Owen reassured him it was a clever buy. He promised to help him transform it. And he was as good as his word, enlisting the help of several cronies. Long-term unemployment had turned them into DIY experts with all the necessary specialities, even plumbing! In a short time they put in windows, installed a bathroom, painted, papered, and furnished throughout with ill-assorted donations.

Between times Dan helped to arrange the wedding and to reassure Rosaleen, who was immobilized by constant headaches and vomiting attacks. She could not believe the drastic revision of her future. Everyone said she would settle down later. Settle down. It sounded mature and comfortable, full of calm pleasures.

The marriage took place. Rosaleen looked brilliantly happy. There was photographic evidence of the ceremony, otherwise Dan might have doubted its reality. Such a swift passage. He was twenty-four and the sudden possessor of a wife, a house, a baby (*in utero*), and one white labrador, Lily, who elected to transfer her devoted presence from Rosaleen's old home to her new one. 'Whither thou goest, I will go.' Despite all obstacles. Dan was clearly an obstacle. Not only was he a rival for Rosaleen's affections, but he treated Lily as an intruder and a parasite. At least at first. Especially as she was a timid creature who had never grown used to explosions and gunfire. She would set up a catastrophic lament on 'busy' nights. But gradually Dan grew fond of her. He liked her frailties. She was unwarlike even with the race of cats and would flee behind a chair at the slightest ominous sound outside. She shunned the company of other dogs except at the times of seasonal passion, when she would manage to outwit the most careful vigilance and escape to copulate with every stray in the district. Despite innumerable partners, it was always the ugliest mutt who managed to impregnate her. Rosaleen had succeeded each time in finding homes for Lily's offspring, either selling them if they inherited their mother's beauty, or giving them away if they resembled the ill-favoured male.

Dan started to lavish Lily with food and endearments, melting her distrust. Soon the poor animal had an amorous dilemma. If Dan and Rosaleen were in different rooms, she would shuttlecock between them, monitoring them in turn, unable to bear the absence of the other for more than a few minutes. Dan exulted sometimes when he saw Rosaleen walking outside with the dog. The girl wrapped in a black cloak, the tap tap of her high heels making an arrogant and secretive sound, the silky white dog tramping beside her, two shy indifferent female creatures. He was proud of Rosaleen. She was superior to other women, especially all their neighbours: the fat women in headscarves, the brazen unhealthy girls, the bored women who went to work, the bored women who did nothing.

It was her lovemaking that made him uneasy. There was a physical readiness in her, something frank and voluptuous. He liked to hold her for a long time with her clothes on. He wanted some resistance.

Rosaleen thought he had no sexual past and he did not disillusion her. But he was used to casual encounters, to lust followed by disgust. The disgust itself had become a pleasure and an absolution. Maybe he didn't feel good enough for Rosaleen? He had had too many tiny lonely untriumphant orgasms. He was afraid of being found out. She was sharp. She said things that humiliated him. Like the time she came out with: 'You always touch me more when we're in company than when we're alone.' She seemed to be cataloguing what was weak about him, things he had no control over or was ignorant of himself.

He tried to talk to her about sex in a roundabout way: 'I'm a screwed up Catholic.'

'What does that mean?'

'I wish you were my sister.'

She looked hurt but she answered him flippantly: 'Oh. I will be then. With occasional lapses.'

End of conversation. She became subdued after that, always waiting for him to approach her. 'That's not what I meant,' he thought. Except it was. In a way.

He reassured himself that it was her advancing pregnancy that had put her off, not his attitude. It would get better after the birth, he decided. It did get better after the birth. But it got worse after the death.


Before Aidan was killed, Dan had found marriage both a burden and a delight. He had lived essentially alone since he was sixteen. It was hard to get used to Rosaleen's proximity. Her 'ways' both irritated and amused him. Her habit of making dozens of cups of tea and then letting them grow cold beside her. The way she fled upstairs if there was a knock at the door. She was like an animal in her lair. Her impulse to flight always overcame her curiosity about the identity of her callers! But the thing that truly bothered him was the way she persisted in wearing her ordinary clothes even in the sixth month of pregnancy, forcing zips and buttons to meet by sheer power of will. The waistbands bit into her flesh. 'Leave me alone,' she shouted at him when he tried to dissuade her. Her eyes were feverish, her skin clammy all the time, as if she were really ill.

During that time they argued almost daily. Their quarrels dared not be personal; they were always about Men and Women. 'Women are such liars.' 'Men have all the luck.'

It hurt and maddened both of them but they could not stop or did not want to. The worst row soured them for a whole weekend. She had read out a newspaper article about women prisoners in some hot hellish right-wing country who were allegedly raped by specially trained alsatians.

'That's anatomically impossible,' he said.

13

'Of course it isn't.'

'You're always ready to believe any far-fetched story about wrongs committed against women.'

'Why should this be a lie? Even if it's untrue that they're tortured in that bizarre way, they are still tortured.'

'The men who are killed, tortured, and imprisoned must out-number the women by hundreds to every one!'

'So? Does that mean it doesn't matter if a woman is tortured? You're saying that I make distinctions . . . But it's you!' She shrugged. 'Anyway, at least men are injured by their own kind . . .'

'Ah! There you are!'

'What are you looking so pleased for?'

'You admitted it! You think women are a separate superior species!'

To register her discontent with that retort, she flung her cup of ever-handy tea across the room, splashing the wall with tea-stains which later proved indelible.

He waited to see if any further acts of vandalism would ensue. He told her coolly that it was a matter of regret that marriage had tempted her to dispense with ordinary restraint and civility.

'That's the sort of bloody elegant glacial thing your mother used to say. According to your complaints! You think you're so unlike her?'

Two days of silence followed. She broke down first, thank God.

Nearer to the birth, pregnancy seemed to lull Rosaleen. She lived in a passive excitement, without thought. Sometimes she mixed up her words, no longer remembering the subject she had been dis-cussing a moment before. Dan became impatient for the birth. He would thrill himself with a litany of girls' names. His daughter must have a strong majestic name: Stella. Lavinia. Charlotte. He would not give her a common Irish name. There was such a surfeit of Marys and Maeves. Perhaps he should call her after an Irish heroine. He admired Maud Gonne, but Maud was too old-fogey and comical. What about Constance Markievicz? . . . No. Let her find her own heroines. She would be born under the sign of Scorpio, which endows its natives with passion, endurance, mastery, a penetrating mind and a lacerating tongue. It favours healers, mystics, saints, and sinners. Dan was satisfied with this information gleaned secretly from a book.

He would teach her to speak as soon as possible. She had so much

14

to learn. It amazed him how anyone ever acquired the stores of knowledge necessary. He would be her guide. He remembered that when he was a child he thought there were several moons because he saw one everywhere he went, in so many apparently different parts of the sky. And his mother laughed and 'Oh Darlinged' him when he asked her the exact quantity of moons but did not tell him the truth. He would not mess about like that with Charlotte. When it occurred to him that he had a fifty per cent chance of having a son, he was filled with dread. Maybe he feared it would resemble him? Or that he would have some magical compulsion to treat him as he had been treated? In November his son was born. As he watched the child's slimy emergence, Dan's female preference was dispelled. He stared at Rosaleen and the baby for a long time. They looked at once unconnected, deeply connected, careless of all connection. She was drowsy with Pethidine. He saw the baby before she did and he was glad. As if he had stolen a march on her. If only there weren't all these 'connections', he thought now.

He fetched Rosaleen a whiskey. 'Here, get it down you.'
'What next?' she pleaded. 'What are we going to lose next?'
'Do you blame me . . . for Lily?'
'No. There's no protection from them, is there? How could you . . .?'
They were whispering. He went to put the dog's basket out with the rubbish.

# 2

Belfast was suffocating. It made him long for open country; some-where to breathe free and deep. The city was flanked on three sides by mountains, a huge cemetery overhanging its north side. Like an omen. Or a comment. He must not keep looking up at the hills. Whence cometh no help. Must keep alert. Trust no one, as he had been warned. He stood at the observation post and watched the milling bodies. The people looked sullen. Or scared. Or just dog-tired. It was late 1979. They had been fighting for eleven years! Sometimes Gerry felt he was in a slum area like any other; sometimes it was like another planet. When he first arrived there, he had gone mad with his camera till he was stopped. ('They'll think it's intelli-gence-gathering, you fool. If you want to take snapshots, come back as a tourist.') But he had quite a collection of photographs, an evangelist wearing a plastic bib covered with a Bible text, 'When the wicked perisheth, there is shouting'; some Orangemen holding aloft a Temperance banner; a wall covered with chilling messages: FTQ, which turned out to be a shorthand exhortation to commit an extra-ordinary act with Her Majesty; 'What's blue and flies through the air? Louis Mountbatten.' It was that kind of raw gloating hatred that frightened him most in this country.

In his first week there was a spate of tit-for-tat killings. Every dawn brought to light some pathetic corpse dumped somewhere. Police and ambulance men would descend quickly to remove it. They looked stonyfaced, accustomed, as if they were sweeping up McDonald's litter. Two of the Catholic victims were killed without resort to guns or knives. Beaten and kicked to death, their faces squashed into mincemeat. Gerry couldn't stop thinking about that. It seemed that mere killing wasn't enough punishment, couldn't assuage that hatred. The assassins had to make the most of it, a prolonged operation. As if with every kick and blow they were saying, 'I mean it! I mean it!' But how could you hate a stranger so much that

16

you wanted to stamp out his very face? Gerry thought that if he had to kill someone it would have to be as quick and neat as possible. Scientific. Any long slow process always aroused doubts and regrets in him, even the wooing of a girl or the reading of a book. So how could those men not wonder in the middle of doing someone in? Why were they not moved by the man's cries? What made them so certain? It was awesome. He wondered how people could endure that level of fear? They seemed resigned to it. 'Murder is respectable in Ireland,' said Des. 'It's sex that's the real shocker!' He made a face of mock horror. 'You know that cinema we passed yesterday? The de luxe fleapit? They're showing a porno film, right?'

'Do you want to go to it?'

'There's a better show outside! Remember all those people we thought were queuing to get in? They're bloody picketing it twenty-four hours a day! They stand there singing hymns. It would be a brave punter that would try and get past them, I tell you. There's even a contingent from the Upward Bound Club.'

'You're making it up,' Gerry said in the middle of a fit of giggles. He was always giggling. Des had to thump him to make him stop.

Gerry had not been prepared at all for Ulster, although officially he was fully prepared. He thought now that being born there might be the only real preparation! He remembered the briefing lectures he attended during his 'internal security' special training, so-called, at Lydd. They were given a potted history of Ireland: eight hundred years of horror and counter-horror explained in three hours. 'Potty' history the officer joked, while the squaddies guffawed obediently. It was like school where you listened not to what the teacher said but to how he said it, so that you could laugh on cue, look impressed on cue.

Anyway, none of the beautifully mapped history made sense now that he was here. He was supposed to be in Belfast to keep the peace. Isolate the gunmen. That was a nice phrase. Made the gunmen sound like some manageable quantity. But they were legion, swarms, unbreakable. And didn't wear any identifying insignia! Every man was a gunman, or a supporter of gunmen. The support was rarely only verbal. Even preschool kids threw stones at soldiers, collected milk bottles for the production of petrol bombs.

So it didn't make sense that he was there to protect the Catholics from the Protestants, which was one of the garbled justifications he had heard. You were safe in Protestant areas. The Catholics were your enemies. There were so many ghastly warnings about them: the story of the hospitable lady who gave sandwiches to some soldiers. The filling was powdered glass. The kids who collected autographs of IRA gunmen . . . They wanted to kill you. They did not want your protection. The Protestants were British like you. More than you. Their houses were bedecked with Union Jacks. There were pictures of the Queen in their parlours. Also Philip, Anne, Charles, Mark Phillips. But not Margaret. She was too flighty.

Gerry and Des went to the Martyrs' Memorial, attracted by the oratorical fame of Ian Paisley. The service began with a few hymns full of stuff about the battle, striving, not resting. A few Jesus jingles. Then Paisley rose.

They watched the black bulk of the man as he paced back and forth, brandishing a Bible above his head. 'This is not a book of peace! This is a book of war! Jesus was no softie! "I come to bring you not peace but a sword".'

A lot of words about hell's busy bonfires that depended on supplies of infidels, sinners and Papists. Hell seemed to be a place built to the satisfaction of Protestants. When the audience was all worked up into a lather, he boomed at them: 'Come, come to the Lord.' Gerry watched the lewd devout faces of the women who were coming, coming to the Lord all right.

Outside after the service the congregation looked like sane and worthy citizens. The Protestants. Our allies. Yet, these were the people who brought the country to a standstill with a general strike in 1974 to bring down a power-sharing experiment. To defy the British government . . . But you were safe in their areas. The Catholics were your joint enemy. At Lydd there was a model ramshackle town nicknamed 'Tin City' where the soldiers had to conduct mock battles and arrests as part of their training. Gerry had enjoyed it. It made the conflict less real, not more, like a Hollywood film set. One of the exercises involved one group of men pretending to be Protestants taking part in a funeral procession while a group of 'Catholics' tried to steal the coffin.

Did Catholics do such things? Why?

There was a lecture on the IRA. Their weapons, tactics, ideology, structure. There were the theorists, Sinn Fein, and the military, Provisional IRA, 'the mouth and muscle ends of the business', the officer said. The IRA had once had a structure which was a replica of

18

the British army with regiments, battalions, titles, ranks, training, and strict discipline. They had now changed to a cellular structure. There were separate independent units each responsible in an area for a single activity: bombings, executions, bank robberies . . . The aim of this was to diminish the amount of information that could be 'extracted' from any caught IRA man.

It sounded clever. The IRA were disciplined, dedicated, and clever. Not as they were portrayed in *Soldier* mag. every week where the cartoon man Seamus could be relied upon to blow himself up or shoot himself by accident. That was as true as an army recruiting ad!

They were shown a film about IRA atrocities. The final shot was of a woman speaking at a graveside: 'We'll bury our sons and daughters and we shall be *proud*.'

Then followed the usual homily by the officer. 'Despite all of this viciousness, the general population continues to support them.'

Des raised his hand.

The officer blinked in confusion. 'What is it, man?'

'Why?'

'Why what? Oh . . . Because a lot of the Irish are mindless fanatics. Easily led by politicians and priests. George Bernard Shaw, and he was Irish himself so he knew what he was talking about, he said: "Put an Irishman on the spit, and you will always find another Irishman to turn him." ' He beamed down with brotherly love on his own compatriots by way of contrast.

'Mindless fanatics,' Gerry thought. 'Mindless. That's what you think about us, too. *Sans* 'O' levels, *sans* everything.'

He felt queasy when he received his yellow card. Licence to kill. It listed the circumstances in which he was allowed to aim fire.

If he identified a sniper or a petrol-bomber.

If his life or another life was in danger.

After giving a warning.

He was to use only one round.

It would take ten minutes to go through that rigmarole. 'Will the other fella wait while I shout, "Halt, who goes there", and all of that? I'd have more holes in me than a bloody colander.'

'Your yellow card is more for your PR,' the sergeant told him. 'Listen, if they've got petrol bombs, shoot them. If you're sure they've got a gun, shoot them. If in doubt, shoot.'

It was nearly the end of his duty when a kid came up to him

grinning widely. Gerry smiled back and the boy ran away laughing in delight. A few moments later, he returned.

'Hey, you.' He stood squarely in front of Gerry.

'Yes?'

'Message for you, Mister.' He pressed something into Gerry's hand.

Gerry gripped his shoulder, making him whimper. The kid flailed and wriggled free. He ran away shouting, 'We'll beat you lot, Mister. No sweat.'

From the corner, he chanted a song: 'Fairy Liquid makes petrol bombs stick to your face, stick to your face . . .'

Gerry tore open the envelope to find inside it a creased piece of paper. He read: 'Happy Christmas, it will be your last.'

The kid was jeering at him. A friendly spiteful laugh.

'He wants me dead. It's nothing personal. Not personal.'

A corporal strode over to Gerry, face swollen with rage. He had the look of some minor official whose authority has been flouted.

'What did I tell you? What did I tell you *repeatedly*? Do not let them hand you anything. It could have been a letter bomb. You are lucky to be still stood there.'

'Yes, Sir. Sorry, Sir.'

Gerry looked away from the corporal's reproachful eyes to the kid's mean face. It was hard to appreciate his good fortune.


'It's a soldier's duty to keep himself fit!' he thought, recalling the officer's carping voice. 'Some chance.'

He frowned at the greasy fried eggs and the grey porridge. All the food was disgusting. Overbright tinned vegetables, powdered potatoes, meat that dogs would gag on.

'Fit! How can I keep fit? Fit for shit.'

He made his way towards the table where Des was sitting with Shiner and Jock, who was already shovelling spoonfuls of the muck into his jaw. 'How can I fit in with this bloody mob?'

Des noticed Gerry toying with the food.

'It's the acid test.'

'What is?'

'If you can stand the nosh, you can stand anything.'

Shiner sniggered. 'I could stand some of that there, no trouble!'

20

He pointed his fork at the Naafi waitress. 'Cor, I'd drink her bath-water, I would.'

Gerry glanced at the object of Shiner's loud-mouthed lust. A young shy girl with drab hair. She was gathering up used plates, avoiding the men's eyes.

'Poor bitch,' he thought. Not that he wouldn't mind a go at her himself. Not that he hadn't itemized her ordinary charms. He was randy as hell. It was something to do with the talk, talk, talk, about sex. The lack of women. The danger of death. Yes. The nearness of death made him feel what he felt. The possibility of death. The impossi-bility of life. Anyway, he was sick of Shiner's 'tireless prick' act. He was sick of Shiner. A real DIY merchant, always pulling his wire beneath blankets. A very *common* person, Gerry decided. He grinned. Common. His mother's favourite adjective.

Gerard Harris. Uncommon common soldier. The late Gerard Harris. Only son of . . . Working-class hero of immense plans. Of gigantic galactic-wide plans. Dead. Fled. 'We regret to inform you . . .'

'Give us a fag,' Jock demanded as Shiner lit himself a smoke.

'Naw.'

'Give me.'

'I'm befucked if I'll give you one of my fucken fags. Not after you wasted all yours stubbing them out on that Paddy we hauled in yesterday. Just to make him squeal! Scotch sadist!'

'Aye, and he did squeal! He was ready to shop his own mother.'

'Jolly good show, old boy.'

'Aw, give us a fag. I've forgot my cash.'

'You'd forget your tiny prick if your hand wasn't always on it!' Shiner switched to an officer's upper-crust tones: 'Let me explain.' He held up his rifle. 'This is for making Paddy croak.' He clenched his fist. 'This is for making Paddy sing.' He held up his cigarette. 'This,' he inhaled and blew smoke into Jock's face, 'is — '

'Fuck it!' Jock slammed his fist on the table.

Shiner grinned with satisfaction. Gerry held his breath. He could not understand why Shiner was always baiting Jock, and why Jock let him. Jock was a hard-faced Glaswegian, a real double-Y chromo-some heftie who looked as if he'd slug you if he didn't like your face. But he was powerless with Shiner.

There was silence for a moment.

'Did you hear about the Paddy who blew himself up last month?'

Gerry shook his head cautiously. It might be a joke. It might be for real. 'Blew himself to smithereens.' Shiner was eyeing Jock. It was another needling exercise. 'A real Irish stew. We had to pick up the pieces, as it were. Guess who turned green? Or should I say yella? Who puked his guts out? Remember, Jockie? The skull? Split in two like a coconut. Brains all over the place . . .'

'Gentlemen,' Des interrupted. 'We've been misled. Your Irish aren't supposed to have brains!'

Jock barked with laughter and relief. They all joined in.

The officer stood on the podium, hands behind his back. He spoke gravely. 'You are going to be shown a photograph of every inhabitant of this district. It is your task to get to know these faces, every one of them. It is also in your interest. Then you will be alert to mysterious absences. You will be instantly aware of any strangers entering the area.'

A succession of mug shots began. Old men and women with thick white hair and stubborn mouths. Tough young men in rumpled jeans or suits. Ageing girls. Plain, hard, closed faces. Children, many children. And babies. Babies in women's arms. Babies in children's arms. Each adult's name, address, age, job, and criminal offences were read out. Few had jobs. Nearly all the men had criminal records. The list was amazing: membership of the IRA, possession of firearms, rioting, car theft, fraud, robbery, transport of explosives . . .

Photographs of jailed relatives and people on the run were also shown. These were the men and women who had maimed and murdered . . .

Streetloads of lawbreakers!

'Study them. Get to know each face.'

Every time a girl's face appeared, the soldiers whistled and roared. Gerry was ashamed. Why the hell did they have to behave like that in front of snotty officers?

Anyway, the girls were not beautiful, he judged. A load of council house lookalikes. Same as the girls he had always known.

'Daniel Keenan,' the officer spoke, showing the gaunt tired face of a young man. 'Medical student, twenty-five years old, clean so far, but some dubious connections.'

Next a girl's face. She was different. Gerry stared. The pouting

22

mouth of a suffering child. Eyes full of unwillingness. Unwilling knowledge. Adult knowledge.

'We are not like other people,' he told her silently.

'Rosaleen Keenan. Nineteen . . .'

His sister?

'Wife of Daniel Keenan.'

There was nothing foolish about that face. Oh why the hell should he pay attention to her face out of that whole library of faces? Anyway, he didn't like her old-fashioned hair, parted in the centre and hanging down like two limp curtains. Didn't she look like one of those haughty rude girls who think they have the right to be boring? Another slide. Another. A twenty-year-old widow with a bright holiday-snap smile. The place was full of widows who were too young even to be wives!

Rosaleen. Wife of . . . couldn't recall the man's name.

Rosaleen.

When the parade of street faces was over, the officer said, 'Well, men, I could not fail to notice your approval of the womenfolk!'

He smiled at them for all the world like an old pimp. 'Here are two more beauties for your inspection.'

The routine whistling broke out. The officer held up his hand like a traffic policeman.

'In March last year these young women met two off-duty soldiers at a party on the Antrim Road. They were friendly. Exceedingly friendly . . . They invited the soldiers to a private house, where they might be free to . . . extend further hospitalities towards them. The men went. Later, when their defences were down — along with everything else — one of these lovelies emptied a Sten gun into them.

'Women, in this country at any rate, are as ruthless and as vicious as the men.'

He went on and on about the number of women active in the IRA, the number in prison for terrorist offences. It sounded like multitudes.

He showed a slide of an IRA funeral march. Women were flanking the hearse. They were all wearing black glasses and berets. Gerry could not recognize any of them. But they must be the same women he had seen earlier, the same everyday faces. Now they were transformed. Glamorous. Sinister. Was Rosaleen there? Would she let her hair fall loose or would she cram it inside the beret?

23

He knew what it was about those women. Despite their men. And their extravagant loads of babies. They were no one's property. They belonged to their own passion. The passion of hate. Rosaleen was no one's wife. She could not be anyone's wife.

Another slide. A young woman tethered to a lamp post, her head covered with some oily liquid, her full breasts partly bared by a rip in her shirt.

'This is Marta O'Hanlon.'

'Ohhh, I'd love to martyr her,' Shiner whispered.

'Her hair was cut off by a group of women. They poured red lead over her head until it dripped into her eyes. Men ran their hands over her body and urinated against her while women cheered them on . . . Her crime?' He paused for several moments, looking round the whole audience, then spoke: 'She fell in love with a British soldier.'

Another slide. A group of smiling women, arms linked.

'Charming picture. Look as if they're playing ring o'roses, don't they? In fact, they are trying to prevent ambulance men from rescuing an injured soldier.'

The silence in the hut was total.

Lloyd suddenly crashed into the room. 'On the street, you two. Bit of bother brewing. Bring the perspex.' Gerry grabbed his riotmask, flung his rifle over the shoulder, and lugged the transparent shield downstairs and outside.

When he looked at the scene, he felt stupid. Rifles, shields, armoured cars on the one side. On the other, a horde of shouting women.

'What's up with them?' he asked.

'We lifted some young lad last night. The bitches are sore about it.'

The women kept up a chorus of abuse. Some of them spat great gobs of yellow phlegm, and they must have had plenty of target practice. Suddenly one old hag dashed forward and clawed at the sergeant's face. He half-laughed, 'Hey, hey . . .' and pushed her back.

Her face turned righteous red: 'Hit a woman, would ye, ye wee bastard?' She charged at him again. He knocked her down.

The women surged forward, cursing and shrieking. Gerry was scared. Their voices were like one voice. Their shouts were not yells of fear. They were the screams of total refusal. The same scream that was inside him when his father died a few months ago. He stood there dumb and useless until they began to jostle him.

'Aw go home. Get home, all of you,' he shouted.

'This is our home,' a voice came from the other pavement.

Rosaleen. He recognized her at once. She stood there, proud and calm. He had a sudden shaming awareness of himself. His bulky uniform with its moronic painted leaves. His shorn hair. Black-rimmed nails. Clanking weapons.

*Our* home. He looked at the broken pavements, foul puddles, ice, mud, poor crumbling houses. The whole ruined landscape. To her, he and his fellow soldiers were the only eyesore in it!

Rosaleen blushed at his stare. She looked awkward and young now. Ignoring the pleas of the women to join them, she walked away rapidly.

A woman was wagging her finger at Des: 'We'll get you. Your days are numbered. Easy to pick you out, Blondie, with your hair. Look at his hair, girls! Like an albino rat!'

The sergeant ordered the water-cannon to be used to clear the street. A volley of water pelted the women, drenching their hair and clothes. They scurried away.

'That's flushed away the shit!' someone said. 'Next time it'll be purple dye, you whores!'

He slumped back on the bed. Tuller's cat, Sheba came and nestled close to him. He stroked her, glad of the animal's warmth against his chest. It was a big velvety mouser of a cat that Tuller had stolen on a house raid.

Suddenly the cat was snatched away. Gerry opened his eyes and looked straight into Tuller's fat furious face.

'Leave my fucken tabby alone. It's mine, M-I-N-E, understood?' He walked away, petting the cat as if it had been molested.

'I'm as good as anyone,' Gerry thought. 'As anyone on earth.' Tears burned his eyes. There were too many rules. Rules for inside. Rules for outside. So many ways of giving offence . . . Suicide impractical . . . You'd never be alone long enough! There was no one to outlive him. No one of any importance.

The room pressed in on him again. There was a smell. His own smell? Or something spilled? Sunk into the floor? Rats' droppings?

He remembered the woman yelling at Des. 'You albino rat!' Des's

25

face. Grey. Ill. Des could not manage. This was more than Des could manage! Gerry groaned out loud.

'Shut it, Chrissake!' Tuller rapped out.

H-Block can't be worse than this, Gerry thought. 'We have nudes on the walls instead of shit, that's all. Horny Block.'

He surveyed the naked women. Moist mouths, plump tits and buttocks, assorted orifices. One huge picture of a woman, her legs parted to show her cunt, purple and glistening like bruised fruit. He stared at her. Her eyes were dead.

Her nipples had more character. They confronted you more than her eyes. Rosaleen ... If Rosaleen were caught naked ... If he surprised her, dressing. Or bathing, say. She would freeze over. Like an animal. Her hands would stay at her sides. She would *stare back*. Rosaleen ... Rosie.

Gerry looked scornfully around him. Some disco! It was a drinking hole. The music was tinny. The microphones did not work properly. Nobody cared. Shiner was there, Shiner was always everywhere, the fat waster. The man would not shut up. If he ran out of words, he gave a royal belch and shouted 'Pard'n me'. He bellowed, he drummed his fingers on the table, he pressed large tips on the barmen.

'Why the fuck did I come here?' Gerry wondered.

Shiner started on his bombing stories. He had done a tour during the worst of the bombings in 1972. He dripped with nostalgia when he spoke about it.

'There was this guy, right? Half blown away, you know? One side intact. Perfect as you or me. Well, as me. And your other side, nothing! Clean blew away.'

Tuller began to sing 'Yesterday': I'm not half the man I used to be ...'

'We couldn't get Jockie a prick transplant out of it.'

'Fuck off,' Jock said dully.

'Look at Harris,' said Tuller, 'ogling the women.'

'We thought you was a bumboy,' Shiner jeered.

'Oh, I am,' Gerry said, 'but it's nothing for *you* to worry about, duckie.'

Tuller squinted at the dancers. Girls in nylon anoraks and high-heeled shoes. Black silk pyjama trousers and tattered running shoes.

'They need a good fucking, those Irish tarts,' he muttered. 'A proper fucking.'

'Fuck *à l'anglaise*,' Shiner suggested. Everybody laughed.

The more they drank, the more they put their arms around each other. 'True friendship,' Gerry thought sourly.

He staggered to his feet and made his way across the floor.

'England expects,' Tuller shouted after him.

The musicians were at ease now, in command, jackets off, sleeves rolled up, faces shiny with sweat. The lead singer flicked his hair out of his face. Gerry wished he still could do that! His face was too naked, too open.

A girl, any girl. *The* girl. 'I choose you. You are chosen,' he thought, steering her on to the floor. Short red skirt. Matted blonde hair. She swayed like a drunk. Her feet went thumpety thump thumpety thump. God, what a peasant! The band went into a slow smoochy number. The girl slid into his arms like a familiar lover.

Her hair smelt like blankets. Her hands were wet. She was easy. He could do anything he wanted. He knew it. From her bare white arms, from the way she tilted back her head . . .

Gerry caught sight of the singer. He was watching them! Wide mocking eyes watching him with the girl!

Fuck the Irish! Fuck them and their secret private smiles!

He looked at the girl's face, surprising her. 'Irish men piss on soldiers' tarts,' he remembered, and in that moment, desire flooded him. His prick stiffened and twitched like a divining rod over sudden water.

He moved her towards the exit. Easily. Like pushing an armchair on castors.

She snaked her tongue into his mouth. A good start.

See how I am forgetting you, Rosaleen.

He reached up for the waistband of her tights.

'Oh, don't . . . I . . . it's not safe.'

'I'll look after you.' His voice was harsh.

He decided to work on her from the top end.

Sperm spilled, babies born not my concern women must weep men must . . .

If in doubt, shoot.

She jerked away from him, smoothing her hair.

'How long have you been in Ulster?'

'Too long.'

'Where are you from? What part of England?'

Jesus, interview-time!

Maybe it was a case of 'I'll let you do it but first we pretend we know each other'? Or maybe she was an Irish saint after all?

'Are you a Catholic?' he asked, forgetting that she could not be.

She was indignant. 'Do I look like one?'

He thought, 'You all look the same to me.' It was what you said or thought about black people.

'What do Catholics look like?'

'I can pick them out anywhere,' she said proudly. 'Their eyes are too close together, it makes them sneaky looking, so it does. They're idolators, they're living in darkness.'

Darkness. The dark Rosaleen. Dark girl.

She was dumb, incredibly dumb.

'I have to go.'

'Oh.'

'See you around.'

'Suit yourself.'


Mark Sloan was nineteen years old. Worked as a store detective in a posh shop in Bradford before joining up. Never talked about his former job, but he had the sort of vigilant law-abiding face that suited a thief catcher. Girls probably went for him, although he had funny teeth. Looked good so long as he didn't smile. Engaged to a girl in Bradford. Proper full-scale engagement, complete with ring. Picture of her beside his bed. Muriel. Muriel and Mark. Like a lot of shy people he went in for quiet corrective ironies, especially in the company of excessive people like Shiner. For example:

Shiner: 'We must plan this little fiasco in advance, lads.'

Sloan: '*Advance* planning, eh? That's new.'

What else? . . . He ate in a precise systematic way: all the potato first, then all the meat, item by item. Didn't drink much, talk much, or overdo anything. His personality didn't crash over you in great waves. In fact, Gerry hardly thought about him at all until he was shot dead. In their fifth week. Then he went over everything, dredging up every fact, every snatch of conversation he could remember. As if the assembly of facts would explain something. Like why him. Stupid. It was all stupid. A nineteen-year-old man, over and done with, to be buried in the ground, Union Jack draping the box. To be removed before the drop into the hole. Reusable. Future occasions. Mark lying in the ground. In sure and certain hope . . . Awaiting resurrection. Reincarnation. Archaeologists.

Gerry was full of a sneaky secret joy that it was Mark and not him. Made him feel bad. He saw that joy in other faces too. Also a sharp fear. They were in a row of skittles. He knew it for the first time. Des took it hard. Shortly after the event a corporal appeared in the hut, to gather up the belongings, strip the bed. The picture of Muriel was placed in a plastic bag along with Mark's crossword puzzles, pens, shaving kit.

'You know what that's for, don't you?'

'Stop us nicking anything.'

Des got to his feet. 'Oh no, no . . . In case we get jumpy. They want him deader than dead. Remove all trace.' He walked over to the window. A small fly was moving across the dirty pane. Des crushed it with his fist. 'Why should a fly be allowed to live?'

In the following days, Gerry woke up every morning to see Des sitting upright in his bed opposite smoking. His skin was yellow. Eyes puffy like a drinker's.

'What was it like when your old man went?' he asked suddenly one day when Gerry was washing.

'Not a lot of fun,' Gerry said, pausing before rinsing his face. 'Terrible.'

'I never liked Mark much. I mean, I didn't dislike him. Just . . . we weren't mates. As such. Oh God, why do I have to think about it all the time? I keep seeing him. I mean, mistaking people . . .'

Gerry towelled his face, kept on drying himself more than necessary. 'My dad used to get on my nerves,' he said at last. 'Especially when he came home from work! He hated me being unemployed. Blamed the System, of course, not me. He used to come in all virtuous and deserving, you know, the noble breadwinner. He deserved his choice of TV, the best chair, second helpings, agreement with his opinions, an audience for all the history-making events on the shopfloor that day. But Jesus, after he died . . .'

'Yes, after.'

'He was a good driver, you remember? It makes me think sometimes . . .'

'One way of beating the System.'

Des did not raise the subject of Mark again. He dried up about everything. Mooched around. It was a strange reversal in their friendship: Des had always been a toughie. He moved into another hut to get away from Mark's bed. Gerry wanted to be private too. He thought of nothing but Rosaleen, her face always before him. He rehearsed conversations with her. About Mark, his father, life, everything. The gap between these imaginary talks and the only real one made him miserable. He re-lived it constantly, that morning he had seen her on the wasteground, picking her way through the mess of tin cans and used plastic bullets, bending to inspect something.

He starts moving towards her, knowing the madness of walking out in the open so exposed, every window like a witnessing eye.

She is crouched over a dead dog, kneading and rubbing its body. She is crying, talking to herself.

'Is it yours?' he says.

She looks up, face hardening at once.

'It's the young lads,' he tells her. 'Target practice. There's nothing we can do about it.'

She will not look at him.

'They're heartless, killing harmless animals.'

'Oh, you'd know about heartlessness!'

'Yes.'

Now she looks straight at him. A look that takes his measure, rejects him. He knows he must keep her here. It is as if he has carried a great weight across the wasteground that can only be relieved by speaking to her.

'I'll have the dog moved. Buried, if you like?'

She makes a sound of laughter that is full of hatred, weakness, and pain. 'Oh take it . . . take every bloody thing away from us!'

'Wait . . .'

But she runs away.

Afterwards he thought incessantly about the meaning of her face. Had he seen a softening in her glance? The look of a woman who knows she is wanted, doubts it, tests, knows . . . Rubbish! She hated him. Why would she not hate him?


On the Sunday morning he was posted on the factory roof overlooking the houses when she appeared early with her husband and

30

headed towards the church. He had never seen them together before. It made him sick to the heart.

'He must know thousands of things about her. Everything.'

He raised his binoculars to study their faces. They had the married look. The blank unawareness of each other. Or maybe they were just tired? He noticed Daniel's hand resting on her arm. Lightly. Husbandly. Proprietorially.

He trained his rifle sights on the hand, then upwards to the head, then veered slightly so that he could only see her. That dark hair, white face. He remembered the surprising lightness of her eyes. Black hair. Blue eyes. That strange Irish colouring. He did not want to like any Irish thing, but he could not help it. It was the natural beauty of her, the stiff pride of her ways of standing and looking. Somehow it connected in his mind with the songs he could hear drifting from the pub every night, that made him long to be free from his thoughts and his loneliness. He tried to dismiss them. Sentimental rubbish glorifying death and murder. As if death was something that happened in a book. But it never worked. He watched Rosaleen stop outside the chapel to don a headscarf. Would she have some different face in there? Rapt and reverent like a child? Or just bored?

Oh, she would be just like the rest of them! Her life full of scrutinies of conscience and pious talk, a babble of mumbo-jumbo ... hail Mary mother of God virgin most pure gate of heaven morning star ...

'You're the 'morning star,' he thought.

What was her bedroom like? *Their* bedroom. He pictured it stark, white, plain.

No, it would be full of the signs of *his* presence. And probably choc-a-bloc with cheap sacred images. Pleading cow-eyes of Jesus. Nailpricked Jesus. Witnessing everything. Witnessing ... No! He could not, would not stand it any more! He was like a lovesick kid.

'I want rid of you, rid of you, I want, I want ...'

## 3

Soldier, that soldier. Always looking. 'What is it about you?' she
thought. Oh, crying again. That baby did nothing only squall the day
through. She wished she had listened to the nuns in school always
prating on as if it were a sin even to look at yourself in the bath let alone
allow a man to enter the holy of holies. But their warnings had only
inflamed her; all those words: 'state of nature', 'carnal acts', 'lasci-
vious thoughts'. The joke was that now she could have sex anytime,
was even entitled to it, she did not want it. It was not that she feared
another pregnancy. She knew she could not have another child.
Nothing could live inside her.

When Aidan was killed, Dan showed no emotion, or even
surprise when he was told. Just sat there thinking or pretending
to think.

But she could not stop thinking about it, Aidan's face always in her
inside self, no matter what she did. Did he know he was dying? Did he
think of what he loved, of his past, or was everything crowded out by
that dying? If he lost consciousness when they were torturing him,
was his death real, or did his death not exist until people discovered
him and said: 'He is dead.'

Aidan died. And she would die.

She scanned men's faces. People said the killers were a punishment squad. The killers were here, in the area, maybe even in the
street. 'Nobody I know did that murder,' she told herself. But she
knew it was a lie. She knew the murderers, but did not recognize
them, could not find them out. Because they were the same as
everyone else. You could kill and it left no trace, no distinctive mark.
She began to look for clues. She talked about Aidan to everybody,
asking for news, watching facial reactions.

Dan grew angry with her. 'Stop gossiping around the place. The
police aren't going to find out anything. You'll get us into trouble.'

'Aidan was your friend. Don't you care?'

'That won't bring him back. Look, he was a tout. He split to the Brits for payment.'

'I don't believe that.'

'I'm afraid that what we believe and disbelieve carries no weight round here!'

'I thought you liked him.'

He did not answer.

She hated the waking sounds, the baby coughing, the loud radio news telling how many died while they slept.

She lulled herself with the getting up, dressing herself, then the child. Feeding him always took so long, she was schooled in patience. Listening to Dan getting ready, she could even make out the rasp of the razor against his cheek. Oh, the havoc he would leave behind him! An aftermath of damp towels strewn everywhere, bottles left uncapped. 'Maybe I will let them lie there. Maybe I will never pick up anything again.'

Out in the street, she walked quickly towards her mother's home, past the windows still lighted against the dull morning. 'Why do I always go there? For company. No, to get the baby off my hands, that's the truth.' Her mother preferred children, even other people's.

In the middle of the next street there was a group of people, a shuffling, trampling crowd. 'What is it? What will I do?'

Now she was aware of the heavy awkwardness of the pram, which had seemed so light and gliding a moment before. 'If anything happened, I could not run away.'

'Oh, the funeral. Always these funerals. How could I forget? The baby. Catherine. Killed in crossfire. I do not want to see this. I cannot look away. Little white casket. Carried by the father. Shut face. His face that will always show that afterhurt. Who gave consent to that death? Who said it must be so? Killed by the IRA. Their bullet found embedded in the chest. Couldn't deny it. The leader apologised. In all the papers. Regrettable accident. Army's fault, for they shouldn't be here. The parents must understand. They must, everyone must see it in historical perspective. Oops, sorree, killed your baby. Shame, shame, but no blame, no. Or yes, blame the Brits, the 800 years' tyranny.

'They act in the name of dead Irishmen, future Irishmen. In the name of what does not exist. Little white box. Brass handles. Pretty, so pretty.'

She slammed the door shut just as her mother appeared from the kitchen. 'Whatever's the matter with you? You're like a dose of bad weather coming in the door.'

'The funeral. Catherine.'

'C'mon. Sit down. Don't grieve yourself. It mends nothing.'

She took Rosaleen's baby out of the pram, a rapt and greedy look on her face like someone untying a Christmas present.

'Could have been worse. Could have been your own, heaven forbid.'

'I can't . . .'

'Oh, Childdear.'

Rosaleen went and looked out of the window. She could hardly see the sky beyond the rooftops. 'Childdear. I'll always be called Child-dear in this house. No matter how old I become.'

Her mother began to talk, an effortless, copious stream of words leaving no space for any reply: 'What's the matter with you? You have your home, a lovely child, a decent man, good prospects. There's not many can say the same round here . . .'

'Where's Katrina?'

'Upstairs feeding your grandmother. Away up and keep her company. It'll lift your mind.'

She climbed first to her old room in the attic, where she used to escape from the family that was always astir with easy quarrels, alliances, betrayals. It was once a place to put off suspicion, put off scorn, sit surrounded by the quiet of ordinary things that looked as if they could never be dislodged. But it was different now. Her possessions were juvenile and tawdry. The battered doll with her school tie twisted round its neck, the purple bedspread she had once begged from her aunt, the bottles of cheap scent. The books she had collected for five years. She flicked spitefully through one or two of them, frowning at the underlinings and little notes she had written.

She could hear her mother speaking to the baby in a low murmur. It filled her with hot helpless hatred. Rosaleen lit a cigarette, inhaled deeply. Only one year ago she had resolved this would not be her life! She had been already sated with mothering from looking after her young brothers and sisters. She had often disliked them. Their implacable little wills. Overheated quarrels. Heaps of unloved toys. Insatiable stomachs. Her life was a dreary round of school and home. School meant a solemn accumulation of fact upon dreary fact. Home

34

was an interminable laying out of meals and clean clothes like sacraments, while her mother sat engrossed in her newest infant. Rosaleen would watch her in a mood of irritation. The sight of that rosebud mouth battening on her mother's elongated teat would drive her from the room. She knew the fecund belly would soon bloat again. Despite her mother's supplications and lit candles to the Blessed Virgin, celibate ambitions, and scalding baths.

Rosaleen wondered sometimes if her father was aroused by his wife's permanent debility. He seemed to have such a cool minimal response to the expenses of the bursting household, although he had not worked for twenty years. 'We've been told we're British like it or not,' he would declare. 'If they're so fond of us, they can feed us.'

At night Rosaleen would often hear through the flimsy wall his swift grunting sex. She pictured her mother impaled beneath his busy shoving buttocks. She would turn up the volume on the World Service or stick her nose into a Charlotte Brontë novel where people were rocked by passions but could be depended upon not to disrobe.

Sometimes she felt sorry for her parents. They often had rows which were probably manufactured to aid some sexual forbearance. They were poor people, destined to get poorer. Whereas, she, Rosaleen . . . University was the first stepping stone for her. The nuns were not keen on this ambition, regarding the university as a cesspit of carnal temptations and revolutionary politics. They were busy with their annual dragooning of their meeker girls into the women's teacher training college, St Mary's, or the convent. The latter was only for those with a genuine vocation, of course, they would emphasize, scanning the room for the wistful faces of future postulants.

No opportunity was lost to extol their own chaste and exemplary lives. The renunciation of fleshly love was nothing compared to their exalted happiness. Their eyes would glisten when they called themselves Brides of Christ. 'The riskless love affair,' Aidan called it, when she parodied their soulful recruitment speeches. She was brave in Aidan's company, relishing his easy scorn of Catholic ritual and belief, the winning authority of his arguments. But when she was alone, her loss of faith frightened her. Her head was always buzzing with questions: 'How could a merciful God allow the suffering of children? How to reconcile the doctrine of original sin with the boundless free will that could land you in everlasting hellfire?' For a while she was beguiled by the Pascalian 'wager'. One must rely on instinct and intuition, not reason. If you were right, you would earn Paradise at the end: if you were wrong, if there is only darkness, you had nothing to lose anyway.

Aidan jeered at the idea of this gamble. 'You think there are no pleasures? You won't catch me trading in a sure thing for a promise of any post-mortem satisfactions!' She felt he was right. But Heaven and Hell, God and the Devil were real entities to her. She could not shrug off the conviction of a fierce, sternbrowed God, ever vigilant over her deeds and thoughts.

The nuns offered one choice. You could either turn your back on the world and serve God. Or safeguard your virginity like some white incandescent jewel to be relinquished to the one and only lifetime incumbent. Bow down to the stupidity of nature and breed. Even Macha yielded. Proud Macha, Rosaleen's favourite legendary queen, the red-maned fearless slaughterer with the power to bind souls. She woke a sleeping king with her lance. At once he was enthralled, but she was unimpressed. Tied his hands with a pliant branch from the weeping willow. So it was with the next besotted suitor, and the next. But finally, she succumbed to some laughing impetuous youth. Even Macha.

Rosaleen set her heart against sacrifice. Church, family, country, were like so many voracious mouths.

'Only the dumb succumb,' Aidan joked once. 'Except your shrewd little sister. She's making a good bargain. McGuire won't be long before he starts his discreet little adulteries, but so long as he foots the bill, Katrina will learn to tolerate it.'

'She loves him!' Rosaleen replied in an impulse of loyalty.

'Love!'

'Don't you ever love your girlfriends?' She could have bitten her tongue out at her lack of sophistication.

'No!'

There were often these spasms of enmity between them, when without warning he was like a member of some other alarming race. She remembered the nuns' armoury of warnings about men; their 'cold unscrupulous search for sensation'.

'You're crammed with romantic nonsense,' he said. 'Don't you see all around you what happens? Fusion! Disillusion!' He slammed his glass down on the table as if to set a seal on his words.

When she sat sulking and silent, he teased her:

'She doesn't drink, she doesn't pet
She doesn't go to Queen's yet.'

Queen's University, that dignified building fronted by a forbidding matronly statue of Queen Victoria, her hand upheld as if to dissuade entrants. Rosaleen was stiff with fear at the thought of rubbing shoulders with Protestants, with so many men, with those English professors of such monumental knowledge and poise. But oh, she would go! It was a comfort that Aidan would be there, just one year ahead of her.

But it was not so easy to devote herself to study. There was no peace, no time. After all the chores at night, when she finally started to read or memorize some drab fact or other, one rasping little cough from another room, the sudden blaring of the television, was enough to send her into near frenzy. The print would blur, she would fling the book aside and sob in despair. Her brother, Leo, goaded her with an unwearying malice about her academic efforts. 'You're afraid of me showing you up,' she told him. She was galled at having to tend the family while he had such privileges, for he was allowed to stay out, no questions asked, and he had always some grubby, silent girl in tow.

She remembered her first and only defiance. Leo came home one evening when she was ironing clothes.

'Hey, get us something to eat, will you?' he said.

'You paralyzed?'

'Look, I've got a bundle waiting for me down the road.'

'Congratulations! Why don't you get her to service you?'

'You're jealous. You couldn't get a fella. Unless you go down the blind home.'

She ignored him, but he came and stood close to her. 'Playing the Christian saint again?'

He ran his hand caressingly over her hip: 'Turning the other cheek, is it?'

In one swift irresistible movement, Rosaleen wrenched the iron from its socket and lunged at his face with its hot underside. Veering, he received the blow on his shoulder. The iron clattered to the floor, as they stood clenched and glaring, holding each other at bay, their nails sunk in each other's arms.

'Why don't you fucken leave me alone?' she spluttered.

'Because you're my sister. I'm sick of you looking down on me.'

She had a sudden desire to kiss him on the mouth. 'Let me go,' she yelled, and ran coatless from the house.

On her return, she announced to her mother: 'I'm not looking after *your* family any more. I won't have him lolling about while I skivvy. And Katrina never lifts a finger except to doll herself up.'

'But Katrina works all day,' her mother said gently, trying to appease her.

'Aye. Painting her nails and gossiping in an office! I work all day. Do you think school is a holiday camp?'

Her father came home after his drinking spree, florid-faced and surly, and was regaled by his wife with the tale of Rosaleen's rebellion and her 'foulmouthed invective' against the whole family. He gave her the few customary clouts before going off to lie down thankfully. She won because she was capable of caring about something. They were too tired.

She worked hard after that. Dan encouraged her. They studied together in his place. She loved the way she could share a room with him for hours without having to 'do' anything about him, even speak unless she wanted. She gained her clutch of high-grade 'A' levels, more than satisfying university entrance demands. But the joke was . . . The subversive foetus was already planted. Unfair to think that way, of course. It was not the second Immaculate, after all.

Katrina was slowly ladling food into their grandmother, talking in a loud, soapy voice as if to a mute infant.

'Come on now, eat up. That's good. That's right.'

Rosaleen watched her grandmother's mouth gape each time the spoon approached. The mouth was like a bird's mouth, the eyes quenched.

'Here's Rosaleen to see you. Isn't that nice now?'

'She doesn't recognize me. She doesn't know who she is, let alone anyone else. What's it like not to think "I I I" non-stop? A baffled absence of herself. If only I could be Katrina. Katrina cannot be repelled.'

'See you in your room,' she said, fleeing from the mingled smells of soup and the frowsty odour of old flesh.

She brushed her hair fiercely with Katrina's brush even though it was not clean.

'Oh, I wish she would die.'

'Rosaleen!'

'I do. I wish she would.'

'Don't dare say that. I'm warning you.'

'You think the same.'

'Life's sacred. It's a mortal sin what you're saying.'

'That's not what you say when Brits get killed, or RUC men.'

'Help me to do my hair, will you. I'm going out with You-know-who.'

Rosaleen unscrewed the cap from the bottle of hair-lightener and applied the pungent liquid to Katrina's scalp.

'Chemical-head.'

'At least I don't need chemicals for the inside of my head!'

Rosaleen started to cry: 'Listen to her crooning over the child! I hate . . . her.'

'Nobody made you get married. God, your mind veers from matricide to suicide and back again.'

'At least it's a two-track mind.' She recovered at once, wiping her eyes with the back of her hand.

'Look, you have a child now, like it or not. You have to get on with it. Dan's OK. It's not as if he was a terror for the drink, and he doesn't spend his life roaring politics either. Where is the baby by the way?'

'She's got him.'

'You never call him by his name. I've never heard you once speak his name.'

'I didn't choose it.'

'Nor him,' she thought. She remembered her father's sour, secret face. 'This is the way you felt about me, all of us. Now I know.'

Katrina looked at her slyly. 'Hope you're making sure you have no more.'

Rosaleen shrugged.

'There's such a thing as contraceptives. For both sexes. In all colours. Works better than a mouthload of prayers.'

'I won't get pregnant.'

'Wise up. We live in a Protestant land in case it escaped your notice. Welcome to Belfast — the post-pill paradise.'

'Mind your own business.'

'I don't understand you. Just to carry on, to let yourself be carried on. It's terrible. Why don't you rail against things, get your own way? I will, I'm telling you.'

'No, you won't,' thought Rosaleen. 'You'll marry that bastard McGuire. Armchair Provie who acts as if the IRA are his personal bodyguard. Making a fortune because everybody's turned alcoholic. You'll coarsen and grow fat and cackle at men's stupid jokes. And sometimes you'll wonder: "Is this it? Is this all?"'

'I love you,' she said. They laughed and hugged. Rosaleen held on to her sister, wanting to hold the moment.

Katrina stood up briskly. 'Come on. Let's hear some music. I've got a Chieftains record, you know the one, "The Women of Ireland"? You can't beat Irish music.'

'Especially if you never listen to anything else.'

'Oh shut up, you.'

The plaintive harp sounds filled the room.

'You must admit it's beautiful.'

'Yes, but it annoys me, the way lovely songs and poems are written about Irishwomen but we're treated like zeroes.'

'Do you have to ruin everything?'

'There are no important Irishwomen, are there?'

'Aw well, there's always the men of Ireland,' Katrina said. 'Every girl should have a coupla dozen. Pity you're out of the running.'

'You're a sexual snob.'

'Hey, that's your baby bawling its lungs out.'

She walked slowly downstairs, listening to the insistent whine.

'Would you quieten him, Mother? I have to go out. Some things I forgot to get from the shops.'

'Certainly. Mind yourself.'

She hesitated at the street corner, unsure of where to go, then headed up past the church towards the cemetery. When she reached there, she glanced over the wall at the crumbling gravestones, unafraid in this half-light. There was a man and woman tending a grave. No. What? There was a kind of trolley beside them heaped with Christmas wreaths and stones? Yes, marble chippings. The man was chiselling at a headstone. She remembered what she had heard about the thefts and desecrations that took place. She did not move. The woman glimpsed her and spoke to the man. They made their way unhurriedly towards the other gate. Rosaleen went to Aidan's grave that was shadowed by the moving trees.

Aidan Heaney: 1957–79.

'You're crying again.'

'What the hell–'

'Don't run away. I won't hurt you.'

'You'll never get the chance.'

'Was he a relative?'

'No. A friend. Why?'

'A mate of mine was killed. Two weeks ago. His name was Mark. He was shot through the head.'

'It's a waste of time questioning me. I know nothing about it.'

He raised his hand in a swift, impatient gesture. 'I'm not asking you anything.'

She felt sick and high. It was as if that soldier's body was lying close to them like some dreadful whispered secret.

'What will happen?' she thought. 'Nothing can happen. It is impossible for anything to happen. Oh God, something *must* happen . . .'

The soldier was looking at her closely and she dared not look back. She thought about the distance from the cemetery to her parents' house, the distance from their house to hers.

'Life goes on, I suppose,' the soldier whispered.

'It's death that goes on and on . . .'

She saw his hand reach out to touch her sleeve.

'Go. Go away,' she told him, but so tenderly, the sound of her voice shocked her. 'You know what they'd do to me? Just for talking to you?'

'He wouldn't want me then,' she thought, 'if they tarred me, if they feathered me, cut off my hair . . .' She started to laugh. 'You wouldn't, would you?'

'Fuck them! Fuck all of them!' he said and she could hear his breathing. His face blurred. She supposed she was crying. Suddenly she was pulling him towards her.

'Oh Christ, oh Christ,' he kept saying. It was as though someone in a dream were praying in her ear. All through their love-making her body was like a mouth filling and filling itself. Her limbs were slipping away from her, out of her control.

'Oh no, no, this body is mine. Am I doing something? Am *I*?'

Her eyes stayed open and it was the same day and the same place, but with every thrust inside her she was getting back and back to . . . what?

41

He withdrew too fast, soaking her thighs. He tried to fasten her clothes, but he was trembling.

'If I look at you, I'll go crazy,' she thought.

'How will I see you?' he said. 'I've got to see you again.'

He was planted in front of her, an obstacle. The stickiness between her legs made her want to scream.

'Leave me alone! Oh, please go away!'

'Thank you, Ma'am.'

She looked straight at him then, at his angry begging face.

He turned and ran. She watched him disappear towards the barracks, like watching a film in hell.

'How can I go home?' she thought. 'Trudge round shops, open packets, make meals? Yes, you can. Nothing happened. I did nothing. No. This cannot be undone. You are in me.'

Shaking uncontrollably, Rosaleen weaved her way through the head-stones and out to the roadway. No one was around.

'I have forgotten what to do, how to get back . . .'

Dan's meditative voice came into her mind: 'Think matters over, take everything into consideration, make various decisions.'

No, move, move towards the house. God. She would not pray. God was the sense of being watched.

The sky the lidless eye of God the sky . . . be sly and lie lie every time you open your mouth lie come lie with me and be my love lie every time you open lie with me open with me . . .

'Oh God, I want a bath. Before Dan comes home.'

Outside her parents' home, she paused to smooth her hair before walking down the hallway into the living room. It was a relief to her that only the glow from television and fire lighted the room. Katrina's head was festooned with curlers which cast a gigantic spiked shadow on the wall. In silence, Rosaleen went past her and through to the bathroom, where she inspected her drained face in the mirror. Before going down to the kitchen, she cooled her features with water and practised a smile. She could only manage a petrified grin.

Her father was standing beside the sink. Rosaleen flushed at his scrutiny. They did not greet each other.

'Mother, I'd better get home quick and make a meal for Dan.'

'Was the shop closed?'

'What? Oh yes. No, no, but I forgot my money.'

'Well, never worry. There's plenty in the cupboard. Take what you need.'

Her father interrupted: 'Are we feeding them as well? Isn't it about time they fended for themselves?'

Her mother answered with tired entreaty: 'Don't fuss. You won't go starving.'

Rosaleen took the food in dumb acceptance. 'Is the baby asleep?'

'Oh yes, he's been as good as gold.'

Rosaleen lifted him gingerly, almost loving the smooth long-lashed eyelids.

In the street she pushed the pram along hurriedly. 'I'm the good as gold mother of the good as gold son,' she chanted silently to herself in unison with the rhythmic squeak of the wheels.

As soon as she reached home, she rushed upstairs and ran the water for a bath. She looked at her discarded clothes on the floor, scooped them up and threw them into the bath.

In the tepid water she soaped herself and her clothes fiercely, unable to get rid of the smell of the cemetery. She remembered walking once with her mother through the graveyard, when she was a child. The sudden cold tickle of horror as she imagined contamination leaking from the buried bones. 'Will everybody die, Mother?'

'It's not real death. We go to Heaven.'

Aidan's face was before her. His mouth opened to reveal blackened teeth. There was the smell of wet earth on his breath. 'Why don't you die, Aidan? Lie down dead and leave me?'

He knows. He saw.

'No one knows. Who knows? How could anyone guess?' She remembered her father's face bleached white with fury when she came home late after lying in the arms of some stranger, half-scared, half-thrilled, copying the breathless vows and kisses she had seen on screen. He seemed to have some supernatural faculty for knowing when she had been with a man. 'You don't know. I did nothing. I don't even know his name.'

She heard Dan moving downstairs, whistling to himself. She pulled on her bathrobe and went down, fingering the raised patterns of the wallpaper along the gloomed staircase.

'Ros!' Dan's voice tugged at her from the living room.

'Don't wake the child,' she scolded.

His face was chaotic with frowning: 'Is there nothing to eat? We're

43

going to McGuire's tonight, remember?'

'I don't want to. I'm tired. I'm not well.'

'It's the benefit for the McConnells tonight, don't forget. They're trying to raise enough to send them away for a holiday. Give them a chance to grieve for Catherine without being plagued by journalists.'

'Conscience money! No, not even that. They want to stop the bad publicity.'

'Come on, a drink will do you good.'

'I don't need a drink. I need twenty.'

'Well then, be nice to your future brother-in-law. Maybe he'll let you drink yourself into a stupor without charge. He could afford to, God knows.'

She sat close to him, coaxing: 'Dan, could *we* not go away for a holiday?'

'Daren't leave the house empty, you know that. Christ knows what would happen while we were away.'

'I want to get away for a while.' She began to cry hopelessly. 'For good. For ever.'

'Try and cut down on the pills, Rosaleen. They make everything worse. Take away your resilience.'

'Oh, it's my fault. This place is all right, it's me that's defective.'

'Oh, don't twist it!' He sighed. 'I know it's grim. It's grim for all of us. Try and hold on. It is our country, after all.'

'Our birthright!' She started walking about. 'Well, I'm afraid I can only appreciate our birthright when I've had my medicine. Being such a weak specimen!' She took a phial of pills out of her bag, counted out some tablets into her palm, speaking in a sing-song voice: 'One spoonful for Lily, one spoonful for Aidan . . .'

She let the tablets drop on to the floor.

Dan bent down to gather them up. 'I'll chuck them down the toilet some day. Just as well Louis isn't at the crawling stage, isn't it?' He saw that she was weeping and went to embrace her.

'I'm sorry. I'm sorry. Don't touch me.'

He stood back from her. 'You sit down, and I'll get us a meal.'

'Thank you. You're kind.'

'Kind to be cruel,' she thought. 'This is your country. And I'm your cunt.' What was it that journalist had said? Irish women are mere baggage. Oh no, Naomi might turn up at McGuire's tonight scavenging for an article. Delivering her sermon again about the perpetually

44

pregnant women. Once she told Katrina and herself about the year she worked in Peking. In China, if a couple produce more than two children, they may be forcibly separated, sent to work miles apart from each other.

Katrina sneered: 'Thank God *we* live in a free country.'

'Free! Don't you realize it's the same here? The pressure is the opposite, that's all. Priests and neighbours meddling into your sex lives, turning you into biddable little breeders! Spittoons for seminal fluid.'

She felt sick listening to Naomi. It was the way her conversation was studded with references to other lands, exciting friends. She imagined some blazing rumbustious life that made her own seem cramped and cornered. It was true they were all under surveillance. There were no secrets. She remembered how in school, she would receive her essays back from the nuns with red-inked screams in the margins: 'This borders on heresy.'

'The Devil lusts for your soul,' they told her. 'He is endlessly cunning, honey-tongued, watchful. He knows all the tricks of glossy argument. He is the source of doubt. If you have doubts, suppress them. Seek help. Pray for forgiveness. You know it is the Devil trying to ensnare your soul.'

'They tell you to bury your brain!' Naomi said.

Katrina hated Naomi. 'She doesn't upset me,' she was always saying. 'Fat white slug.'

Warmed by the firelight, Rosaleen was falling asleep.

She dreamed of a journey, a perpetual slow travel by a boat that wallowed and dipped. She reached a strange land where she could not speak the language. Her arms ached from the weight of the suitcase, but what could she do? She was afraid to offer money in case it would be too little or too much. She fumbled for her passport but it was nowhere in her pockets. In desperation, she opened her suitcase; her possessions scattered wildly as she searched without success. The faces round the room shone with spite. Was it her accent, her clothes, her ineptitude? Was it because her house was burning down in her absence?

A throng of people was already in McGuire's when Rosaleen and Dan arrived. Katrina was working behind the bar, looking plump and opulent, as if the swaggering prosperity of her moneyed fiancé had overflowed on to her. McGuire hovered behind Katrina, eyeing her with lustful suspicion as she played her teasing, fencing game with the men.

'When's the Big Day, Katrina?' asked Duffy, jutting his red, square face close to hers.

'Oh, you'll know when you get your invitation card.'

'Don't be in too much of a hurry. You can marry too soon, I should know.'

'Better too soon than never!' she laughed.

'How's tricks, Rosaleen?' McGuire spoke in a voice that was two parts mockery to one part deference.

'I'm fine. I want a whiskey.'

'You can have a double. On the house. Just for the joy of looking at you.'

'I'll pay.' She thrust the coins forward and turned away from his dry, piquant face.

'Aw well, seeing as it's your *husband*'s money . . .'

She searched around for Dan, who was already sunk in conversation with some man, so she wandered over to the shadowy corner where the women were herded.

'Squeeze yourself in, dear,' said Mrs Boyle, wiping beer foam from her faint moustache. 'You should come here more often. No harm in a bit of drink. Kills the time.'

'Oh, I'm tired of the same places always. You can hardly stray out of the district. It's like living in a cage.'

Marty Boyle, the eldest daughter of her neighbour, turned a scolding face on Rosaleen: 'One's scope is necessarily limited in a war situation. Our lives have been deliberately circumscribed by our lords and masters for centuries, anyway. You're making a very tiny sacrifice when you think of the people prepared to die . . .'

'OK, I know the catechism, Marty.'

'Never mind her,' said Mrs Boyle. 'She would fight with her own fingernail. The young ones are all wild these days.'

'That's true,' said Mrs Lennon. 'You never spoke a truer word. Did you hear about those lads that dug up the graves in the city cemetery? They smashed the skulls. They were prancing around dressed up in shrouds. Mind you, it will bring a heap of bad luck to them.'

Marty scoffed: 'What's dead is dead. It's the living you want to watch out for.'

'I'm telling you. There'll be a terrible revenge. They'll be called to account.' Her deep, phlegmatic voice was impressive.

'I thank my lucky stars I'm not superstitious,' said Mrs Boyle, leaning back successfully. 'Not that I think those lads should get away scot-free. I think the boys should get the hold of them and beat some human decency into them.'

'They will,' said Marty. 'Soon as they find out the culprits.'

She began to tap her glass with her bitten red nails that looked like tiny broken spears.

'I heard they're going to sort out whoever shot wee Catherine,' said Mrs Boyle.

'Do you mean execute?' Rosaleen heard her own anxious, thrilled tones.

'It was an accident!' shouted Marty.

'He shouldn't have fired across a street full of kids playing. There's such a thing as over-enthusiasm,' replied her mother.

'The possessors of the facts are the ones to pass judgement,' interrupted Mrs Lennon, snatching little sips at her vodka.

'It'll either be a shot through the knee or the head. According to merit.'

'Yes, one good clean shot,' agreed Mrs Boyle. 'Not like the Prods. Some of their punishments would freeze your blood. I won't tell you what they do.'

'I already know. Some wisecrack wrote a poem about it, called "Ode to a Missing Member".'

'They're animals! Some things are just not natural!'

'Have you forgotten what our boys did to Ursula?' asked Rosaleen.

'So what?' Marty's eyes squinted up to avoid her cigarette smoke. 'She was a whore to the entire British army. The boys just reckoned it was their turn to enjoy the hospitality.'

'They fixed it so they would be the last guests,' said Rosaleen, picturing the wet slick of blood curling from the punctured womb.

'Now, you two,' said Mrs Boyle with a strained gurgling laugh, 'that's hardly a very nice topic for young ladies.'

A silence fell on the group. Rosaleen watched Marty looping her hair round her fingers, a listless, wronged expression on her face. 'She's almost the same age as me,' she thought.

'Marty, are you not going with any fellas?' asked Mrs Lennon with a guileless look.

Mrs Boyle answered first. 'Isn't she eating her heart out over that tearaway Donnelly, lying up in the Maze? All the age of him, should be worrying about 'A' levels instead of the salvation of the country '

'Shut up, you!' Marty snarled at her.

Her mother went on, complacently: 'Why could you not unearth some decent lad like Rosaleen found for herself? Give me a bit of heart's ease for a change.'

'Dan Keenan. He's in with the boys, sure! Up to the gills!'

Mrs Boyle cracked her across the jaw. 'Guard your tongue!'

Marty's head slumped forward and she remained that way, averting her face. Rosaleen caught the pungent animal odour of her thick hair. She scanned the faces of the men at the bar, until she saw Dan listening to McGuire, who was giving one of his grandiloquent, blustering speeches. 'Berating some foe or other,' thought Rosaleen. Dan in with the Provos? No, it was nonsense. She knew everything about him. She felt her throat constrict as she watched him. Oh Dan! Maybe they could make some stab at joy? Maybe there was a chance?

The smell of Marty's hair in her nostrils was like a taunt.

'Marty!' she spoke out fierce.

The girl looked up in apprehension. The tiny child-cruel face erased the anger from Rosaleen.

'Look, Ros, I'm sorry.'

'OK.'

'I won't say it out loud again. I lost my head.'

Mrs Boyle leaned forward and whispered as if she was in church: 'Did you see the funeral, Mrs Lennon?'

'Oh yes. I got out of work special. I didn't get over the door to pay my last respects though. You know what Sean said? I'm not providing a peepshow for the general populace! He's so bitter, he's forgotten who his friends are. Mind you, I don't blame them, wanting to keep out *most* people. Do you recall the time I lost my man? My new carpets were destroyed with all that horde trampling over them. And the half of them only came to get stuffing their faces with the feed after.'

'Well, we all have our cross, Mrs Lennon.'

'They say it's the gateway to Heaven.'

'There's some of us will have a very fleeting visit to Purgatory if fair's fair, Mrs Boyle.'

'Yes, and there's others are in for a sharp come-uppance. Anyway, you needn't be peeved about not getting near the McConnells. They let no one in save for close relatives and the priest.'

'And the doctor! I heard that Sean tried to wrench off the coffin lid after they nailed it down. Maire's off her head too. The pair of them won't be comforted.'

'Well, wouldn't it break the heart of a statue to lose such a lovely child?'

'I know. All the size of her.'

'The wee darling wasn't on earth long enough to give her parents any heartache.'

'True. They'll have nothing only good memories. God knows children can be a sore trial. She shook her knobbed toadstool curls and drained her glass.

'Well, you should know, Mrs Lennon, with all that mob of yours living in style over in London. Never darken your door from one year's end till the next.'

'There's rooms ready and waiting! I'm tormented with invitations, fares paid, the lot.'

Mrs Boyle kept an impenitent gaze trained on her friend. 'When are you going, so?'

'Oh, I'm not overly fond of London. You're not safe on the streets.'

Suddenly, the continual shifting of the people at the bar stopped. Three high-pitched whistles sounded somewhere outside. Everyone looked startled, frozen in mid-speech, mid-thought.

'Go on!' screamed McGuire. 'It's a tip-off! Get him out for Godsake!'

It was as if he had galvanized them into life. A group of men moved with one will, bustling out a stranger through the back exit, muttering curses and quick words of encouragement.

'Holy God, who's that?' hissed Mrs Boyle.

'He trains men over the border. He shouldn't keep popping up in Belfast.'

The door sundered open and soldiers rampaged in, tilting their rifles at the crowd. Their faces were wan with fright and fatigue. They looked schooled for death.

'Men over to the wall!' yelped the sergeant. 'The rest of you, don't move an inch.'

The men began to shamble in a lethargic queue over to the far wall, where they bent forward and splayed out their hands. Rosaleen wanted to cry out in shame at their undignified posture. Dan was slouching against the bar, whistling irritably through his teeth. A soldier lunged at him, wrenching his arm, scurried him over to the wall. When Dan was spreadeagled, the soldier struck the back of his shins with his rifle, making him groan.

'Leave him alone!' Rosaleen shrieked.

The soldier turned. It was *him*. They stared at each other, appalled by the recognition. It was like meeting some embarrassing blood relative. Everything in Rosaleen seemed to be rising to her throat. This vision of her husband stooped and dwarfed before that soldier, so easily victorious, upright and important, gave her a primitive surge of joy that made her weak and dizzy. She wanted to disown the feeling. Disown herself.

'He's skipped it!' reported the soldier who had searched the cellars and upstairs.

The troop looked bored now, anxious to leave but trying to maintain some panache. They backed out of the door slowly. 'Thank you for your hospitality,' sneered the sergeant with a faint bow as he reclosed the door.

Rosaleen sank back in her seat. How dare he demean her husband before her eyes? He was their enemy. He felt nothing but contempt. He thought he could do what he pleased to their bodies. He had abused both of them. She ran over to Dan. She felt more bound to him by what had happened than by their marriage.

Later in bed, she lay stroking him hundreds and hundreds of times in a mechanical atoning caress. 'I'll be true to you. I'll never betray you,' she promised in silence.

Marty's words kept nagging at her.

'Dan?'

'What is it?'

'What would happen, what would you do if they asked you to be involved?'

He gave a laughing grunt.

'Dan?'

'Oh, for Christ's sake, they don't *ask*, they don't make requests.' He sat bolt upright. 'What's a man supposed to do? If it's not one fucken army shoving you around, it's the other.' He gripped her shoulders, hurting her. 'You can't argue with guns! They're the big boys! They call the tune round here!'

'Have they asked you to do anything? Have they?'

He collapsed back against the pillow, shielding his eyes. 'No, no, forget it. Let me sleep, will you?'

She could not rest, just lay there listening to Dan's breathing and the intermittent whinny of the fridge. The baby began to cry and Rosaleen dragged herself to feed him. She stroked the fragile blue-veined skull. 'It would splinter like eggshell,' she thought, and wept soundlessly. Until the glassy chimes of the milkman's arrival, she watched over her son as if she was guarding him.

# 4

Dan fingered the two newly arrived bills which he had crammed in his pocket. It was almost laughable that while everyone else was bedevilled by the thought of catching a stray bullet or being carted off in an army raid, he was living in a settled dread of debt. His mother's small legacy had dwindled to almost nothing. His next grant was not due for three months. The final demands were becoming more routine and less courteous. Rosaleen would be mad if she knew they had been existing for the last week on a handout from McGuire! But oh, she did not care to know! She seemed to think that money was provided from some miraculous everflowing source. When he hinted at economies, she would put on the airs of some slothful aristocrat: 'I can't manage without a phone. So what if no one else in the street has one? Is there a statute against having a phone if your neighbour hasn't?'

She was proud of her inability to cook. All her meals were made from expensive packaged foods. He knew this financial crisis was partly his fault. At first it had been a chivalry in him that made him hide the bills. But soon he had begun to resent her for not guessing his trouble, for being blind to his sacrifices of important textbooks, she who was always parading her sensitivities! Well, it could not go on, he would tell her straight out. And he would abandon his studies to take a job. She would not dare raise an argument against it.

He did not call out as he entered the house. When he reached the open doorway of the living room he saw Rosaleen preening before the mirror above the hearth. She was coiling her hair this way and that, trying on sunglasses.

'Like yourself?' he asked, sarcastic.

'Oh God, you frightened me! Why are you home already?'

'It's just a break. I've to go back.'

'How many people have you cured today?'

'Someone died.'

52

'Such ingratitude!'

'Why are you trying on sunglasses in winter?'

'Oh, just for effect,' she laughed, clattering them down on the table.

'For affectation?'

She bowed her head and said nothing.

'You're living in a dream world. It's just as well one of us stays afloat!'

'Oh dear, Captain Keenan with his firm hand on the rudder, fearless eye on the horizon . . .!'

A pale merciless sunlight showed up the chaos of the littered room. Dan cast his eye over the worn shredding paperbacks on every chair, the scattered baby clothes, the pair of collapsed jeans lying on the floor beside spools of thread. Rosaleen stood there, stern and bright, as if she was proud of presiding over this messy kingdom.

'Have you time for lunch? I could make . . .' she faltered, watching his face.

'Christ, how could anyone eat in this pigsty?'

She made some helpless disowning gesture as if the clutter had accumulated itself when she was offguard.

'Oh, it's this house. I wish we could leave.'

'It's a pity I don't have your itch for leaving! I have to leave the hospital, whether I like it or not!'

'No! What's wrong? Why?'

He strode over to the wallcupboard, wrenched open the door to find the heap of accounts. He presented her with the sheaves of bills and threatening letters. She examined one or two, then dropped the bundle on to the table without a word. Dan watched her. He had expected her to shout or cry or . . . Maybe she was trying to make him feel foolish? Or did she think it didn't concern her that they were penniless!

'You never said,' she spoke at last in a flat voice.

'I have to get a job . . . And you can do without a phone surely. You can visit your friends, if you're so fond of them.'

She waved her hand impatiently.

'It's too drastic to give up medicine. You can't.'

'Someone has to make the decisions.'

'I can't believe my ears. I can't believe you're really saying this! Couldn't we borrow . . .'

'We're in debt to the hilt now. No one in their right mind would loan us a quid.'

'Find someone not in their right mind.'

'Look, hasn't it sunk in yet that you have to pay for everything. Not just with cash either.'

He heard her catch her breath. 'I get the message.'

'Makes a change.'

She nodded bitterly. 'You're paying for a couple of nights of fucking with a life sentence.'

'Don't speak to me like that. You can keep your filthy coarseness to yourself.'

'Oh yes, of course, but you can say anything you like to me, and that's permissible, that's OK. You can say that I've ruined your life, and your peace of mind and your illustrious career . . .'

'I never said those things.'

She burst into tears. 'I didn't know. I thought I couldn't get pregnant. I thought I was so different from my mother. I thought I wouldn't inherit her bloody awful fertility!'

The baby began to cry harmoniously with her. Dan went to lift him. Suddenly Rosaleen was plucking at his sleeve, her face penitent and hopeful: 'Why can't I get a job? Sure I'd like to. Mother would look after . . .'

'Trust you to try and offload the kid.'

'Oh, you know that's not why . . .'

'I won't have my son installed in that madhouse.'

Seeing her gasp, he added quickly, 'It's your own description, remember?'

She looked defeated. 'Do what you want. I'll have the phone cut off, as you begrudge it so much.'

'It's not a question of begrudging it!'

She ran upstairs. He heard her howling in the bedroom. The baby was crying its lungs out. 'At least crying is free,' he thought.

His head ached as he made his way back towards the hospital, his shoulders stiffening as he passed the sallow-faced soldiers at the corner. He could not bear to be stopped today. Everything was worse; this was not how he had expected to feel. He had imagined a grave conversation with Rosaleen, leading to resolves and cooperation. He had not meant to be brutal, to pummel her with the facts. As for sacrificing his career, the idea no longer seemed heroic. What if he failed to get a job? He might end up with nothing. Was he looking for an excuse to leave? 'Your father was incapable of commitment. To any thing or person,' his mother had been fond of saying. Was he the same? Feckless. Faithless.

'At least I won't walk out on my son!' he thought.

But what could he do about Rosaleen? He knew their marriage was starting to show all the rancour of a more ancient union. It was not that they did not make love. If you could call it that, for she gave herself with careless shrugging ease as if it did not matter. As if nothing mattered. Once he wondered if she feared another pregnancy, and reassured her that he would always take care to withdraw at the last moment. She acted as if he was calling her attention to some display of good manners. They had sex after rows, but it was never because their anger stumbled over into passion, it was never full of forgetting. It was an insincere truce, a dirty white flag.

How had it happened? Their love had been clear and simple at first. But that was before the pregnancy and before Aidan was killed. He remembered when they were new lovers, the time they went to the West of Ireland for a weekend to escape Belfast. She had been so happy away from the city, delighting in everything. She plundered giftshops, buying a Donegal tweed scarf and beret which she insisted on wearing despite the heat, and a multitude of trash souvenirs including a magical talisman alleged to increase creative powers.

'You're gullible, you,' he told her.

'I am not so. I just like to pretend.'

She was creative enough, for she must have conceived that weekend.

That first night they lay together watching the sky crowded with stars which seemed very near.

'Why are there more stars here than at home?'

'They don't care to show their faces there,' he said, before making love to her under that witnessing sky. Beautiful moments — was that all anyone could expect?

Next day they decided to walk to the Silver Strand for a swim in the bay. They set eyes on no one as they made their way over the bleak moorland, which possessed no trees, no flowers, no birds. Only giant boulders, miles of turf, a brackish slow river.

Dan fell silent in the stillness, but Rosaleen kept chattering on.

'I own this place,' she said. 'All mine.'

'You're welcome to it.'

But his mood broke as they began to descend the valley leading to the village. A mongrel dog emerged from a field and greeted them with ecstasy. It was like receiving a friendly messenger and escort from the village below. They debated over suitable names for him, becoming excited now that they were nearing their destination. They could smell the sea and hear it. In the village they called at a shop for some snacks while the dog waited sorrowfully outside. The shopkeeper scowled as they chose some overpriced goods. He flung their change on to the counter like an insult.

'He's obviously in the pay of the Tourist Board,' she said when they left. 'Do you think he hated our Northern voices?'

'Oh, it's just shopkeeper's habitual spite,' Dan said.

'Maybe he thought we were Protestants, God forbid!'

Dan puffed his cheeks out and glared, trying to look smug and stern. 'Do I look like one?'

'God, I'd hate and disown you if you were!'

'But I'm not. And you love me.'

'Oh, who told you that momentous news?'

'You do, don't you?'

'Well, I'm fairly partial to you . . . Yes, yes, I love you. I love him, do you approve?' she bent to ask the dog.

They reached the empty beach and threw down their picnic things.

'Get your clothes off.'

'But I'm a good Catholic girl!'

'There's no doctrine against swimming!'

'Do you think it's wise to go in there?' she frowned, squinting at the tall sunlit waves.

'Cowardy-cat.'

He watched her as she stripped efficiently, removing the prized beret last.

'I'm going to make love to you after.'

'I know.'

'Clairvoyante.'

He had not swum far before the force of the waves knocked his breath out. He battled his way into a shallower part. But where was Rosaleen? The sun dazzled his sight. He could not trace her. Then he spotted her! Her arms beating uselessly, her face a silent scream.

There was no strength for words when he reached her. He had to fight to turn her wriggling body round towards the shore, so that they could be washed forward, while he held her head from submerging.

He wrapped her in both towels, while the dog circled them making little whining sounds.

Rosaleen sat huddled rocking herself back and forwards, weeping. 'Oh God, it was as if the sea hates me! It hates me!'

'You're safe.'

'It wanted to drown me.'

'You didn't drown. I'd never let you drown.'

Suddenly she screamed out at the water, 'I hate you too!'

The cliffs echoed back: 'Yoo-too!'

'I *hate*! I *hate*!'

'Hate, hate,' mocked back at her.

'Stop. Stop it. That's it. That's enough,' he coaxed until she weakened and let him comfort her.

Dan studied the mess of reconstituted potato, stringy meat, and overbright green peas, before pushing aside the meal untouched.

'Waste,' muttered Farrell through his own clogged mouth. 'Mind you, maybe you're the wise one. I'm worried about the weight,' he said, patting the hooped belly that suspended over his waistband.

'A clear case of oral fixation,' Dan said.

'Oh, shut your mouth, Sigmund!'

'Shut yours!' Dan replied, lifting an iced cake and shoving it between Farrell's pointed rat's teeth.

'Bastard!'

'We'll get him a woman, will we, Dan?' suggested Sean. 'Take his mind off the perpetual feeding.'

The plump body rose and marched off with dignity.

'How about it, Dan? Let's find him a girl. Who would be likely to step out of her clothes for Farrell?'

'You could always write a cheque.'

'You have a very low opinion of glorious womankind!'

'I have a low opinion of Farrell's allure.'

'Still, you're always ready with the bitter tongue, I've noticed.'

'That'll do no injury to your romanticism. If you can spend the whole day dissecting their insides, then chase after them the night full of your daft poems and promises . . .'

Sean burst into song: 'Oh, full of promises and promiscuity I am I am! I make promises to a different class of body from what we slice up. You make me sound troubled by the necrophiliac passions . . . Now there's an idea for Farrell.'

Dan rose. 'Come on, or we'll be late. I've to read some case notes. Cirrhosis.'

'The flesh is willing, but the spirits have destroyed the liver!'

They marched down the corridor, their jokes magically silenced by a critical glance from a ward sister.

'Why do nurses look down on us?' Sean asked. 'It'll be a different story when we're fully-fledged doctors. They'll be queuing up, knickers below knees!'

'You make a fair job of misogyny yourself.'

'Not at all! I revere women. They're better than men.'

'Better for bedding down with?'

'Of sounder moral character.'

'Compared to you, no one would dispute it.'

'Listen! There was this time I was staying on a farm in Wicklow. It was a kind of commune, all organic vegetables and self-sufficiency, you know. It came the time for slaughtering the pig, a great bloated piece of flesh it was. Well, it was the men who went to do it. Automatic it was, no discussion. We slit the throat, horrible! The squeals of it, like a banshee. There was warm blood flooding down my legs on to my boots, and its big milky sodden eyes were on me. We could hardly keep a hold of her, she was like a hysterical hippo! We kept shouting to the women to come and help us. They just stood there glued to the earth, big funeral faces on them. You see what I mean?'

'I'm sure the pig appreciated their sentiments.'

'Don't you think it shows the fineness of women?'

'It shows you're a disgusting pig butcher.'

'Ah, you! So you don't agree with me?'

'Sure, I bow to your superior knowledge,' Dan said, remembering the cold complicity on women's faces at news of soldiers' deaths.

'See you,' Sean said, disappearing into the library.

Dan disliked him for a moment. There was something trivial in Sean with his endless headsex and his bragging stories. But the death of the pig recalled to him his own rabbit-shooting adventures when he still lived in the country with his mother. He never felt guilty about killing them. It happened because the rabbit was *there* and he was *there*.

He felt he was the instrument of a fated death. It used to elate him, the powerful kickback of the rifle butt, the rabbit's slight toss in the air as the bullet smashed it. It was as if that single frozen moment of death separated itself from the headlong dash of time. Is that what killing is for? he wondered. To create such a moment, one moment of dominion over time? But was that all there was to it? One day came back to him, a day when he found that the little body he had shot was ravaged by myxomatosis, the eyes were blinded with pus. The death was already there, and he felt cheated. 'The mark of Cain,' he thought dramatically, then shrugged. 'It was only a rabbit, after all.'

In the ward office he scanned the new admission sheets before fishing out his study case. Always he had the mad fearful hope that his father would one day turn up as a patient. There was so little he could remember about him. Catholic gipsy. Brave impregnator of Harriet Keenan. He sounded to Dan like the sort of person who would have sudden fevers and infections if he fell ill at all, unlike his mother who died of a slow treacherous cancer.

There was so much he would like to know about his father. He remembered the first time he himself had looked at his mother with the heretical thought that she was not beautiful, realizing that it was not her physical charm but her own belief in its influence which wielded power over others. Had his father discovered this? Did he simply weary of living with a work of art? A work of artifice. Did he flee from the love she meted out? He imagined her triumphant gloating look if she were alive to know he was giving up medicine as well as the priesthood!

A performing monkey, she had called him! A performing *manqué*!

'Jesus, I won't leave,' he thought. But what could he do?

The memory of her last birthday pressed in on him. He had agitated for a week, preparing himself to tell her he was joining the priesthood, imagining intimate little confidences between them.

But that morning she did not appear. 'Damn it,' he thought, 'is she going to coddle herself all day in her invalid cell? Doesn't she even want to count her cards?' He ate his breakfast in a fury of impatience, listening for the sound of her stirring.

'I know, bring her some coffee. And her bundle of tributes.'

He prepared the tray lovingly, remembering her silver serviette holder and her Barbados sugar in its special bowl. On a sudden inspiration, he went out to the greenhouse and plucked an orchid to place beside her plate. For a few moments he inspected the total effect, then removed the flower. She would not appreciate anything so easily obtained.

It was her custom to languish in bed several days a week, complaining of mysterious ailments, which would melt away when she decided to 'socialize'. Then she would acquire a sullen dogged energy for the ceremony of dressing, perfuming, drawing on of mascara and lipstick. But the real transformation took place the minute she greeted her friends. Dan was still awed at her skilled vivacity on those occasions, the half amorous tones she would use to the provincial hicks she would later mimic and ridicule.

He knocked and entered the bedroom, full of its smell of sweet confined air. It was crowded with music boxes, 'feminine' trinkets, and frill-edged lampshades; he felt ungainly and out of place.

'For me?' she said. 'Set it down. I'll try some coffee in a moment.'

She examined the handwriting on her letters with mild interest.

'Mother, won't you get up for your birthday? Don't stay in here.'

'I could embrace death on a day like this! Draw the curtains, would you? It chills me to see that bleak sky. I do so hate my birthmonth. January is the cruellest month, if I may correct the poet.'

'You could ask some people here,' he said. 'There's plenty of time for you to get ready . . .'

('To adorn yourself! Adore yourself!')

She laughed and gave him a fond look. 'How sensible of you to be born in spring! Tell you what, we'll have a party on *your* birthday. If I'm better. Oh, I will be better. I promise you I will!'

'Mother, I won't be here.'

She turned away with the air of one hardened to disappointment.

'Oh, I see, you've already devised some festive little plan for yourself!'

'No, no, don't misunderstand . . . I'm going to enter the seminary.'

'Seminary! What on earth for?'

'I'm going to be a priest.'

'Is this a joke?'

'I've thought it over. I've talked fully . . .'

'Not with me you haven't.'

'With Father Morice.'

60

'I'm your mother. Father Morice indeed! That servile smelly old fool! Trailing his stinking odour of sanctity everywhere. Just fancy, my son a priest. Oh, they do so reek!'

Dan knew what she meant. That smell like mushrooms and chemicals, a high tiring sweetness. The odour of unused flesh . . .

'The house will be so empty! Not that you're such sparkling company. It must be this morbid religiosity that makes you so drab.'

'I won't be far away,' he said. 'And then you have your friends . . .'

He bit his hypocritical lip, for he knew she was close to no one. Respectful dislike was the strongest emotion he ever read on her guests' faces. He glanced for reassurance at the heap of cards.

'You're being deliberately stupid! With a priest for a son, I'll be a pariah. You know I'm only tolerated in this town because I'm discreet about my religion.'

He stared at the patterns on the carpet. How could he talk about his religious life?

'You'll only stick it for a couple of years, so why bother? Yes, two years I give it. At the most. I'd wager money on it if I had money.' She twisted her expensive rings round her expensive fingers.

'You don't know. You don't know *me*.'

'Oh, but I do. Blood will out, you see. Blood will out.'

She reached for a nail file on her bedside table and began to shape an already perfect nail. The tiny grating sound made him rise to his feet. He went to the window and stood with his back to her.

'Don't start that, Mother. I'm of your blood, too, remember.'

'I hope you know that his Catholicism was accidental. Converted on a whim, not on account of any theological conviction, he never troubled himself about that, no, he was seduced by all the outward trappings, the music, incantations, candles, robes . . .'

Dan listened in powerless anger to the way she spoke of church ritual. As if it were like some supermarket snare! Or like her own stubbornly preserved beauty.

. . . 'He even loved the censer.'

'Censer, censor,' Dan thought idly, then was startled by a sudden vision of his mother stooping over a fire, burning letters. Burning letters from his father to him!

Yes, it was obvious. He knew his father would not have forsaken him! It was an image so unbidden, so convincing, he could not doubt it 'Bitch, bitch,' he thought, forcing himself to speak calmly.

'If he was such a sensualist, why do you liken him to me, when I want to be a priest?'

'This is just the kind of caprice that was typical of him! A man incapable of love drawn to the ministry of love.'

Dan's head began to pound. 'Who was incapable of love? He loved me! He loved me!'

She went on: 'It's a stern vocation, you know. Will you really take those monkish vows? Forgo sentimental attachments, family life? The joys of progeny are overrated, I grant you. Still, "better to marry than to burn". Your father did not find the two activities mutually exclusive. Nor did he realize that "burn" has no direct object in this case.' She gave him a sharp inquisitive look. 'Do you burn, Daniel?'

'Is it true? Did he betray you? Why did he leave?'

'What is there to explain? "Love fades out from kiss to kiss," as the poet says. How can men desire what they possess?' She looked away, but not before Dan glimpsed her private, anguished face.

'Didn't he ever get in touch, even to ask about us?'

'To ask about you, you mean!'

'Well?'

'No.'

'He must have written. Did you think it best not to tell me, perhaps?'

'I never had the dilemma, Daniel. Oh, what's so surprising? He grew tired of you, too. First I was his showpiece. Then it was your turn. Oh, he loved taking you out. Getting you to sing at parties, all that nonsense! Like a performing monkey. A little pet monkey.'

'No,' he sobbed, not caring to hide his tears from her.

Prize cunt and pet monkey? No, it must not be so.

His mother shrugged. 'It's best you shouldn't glamorize . . .' She looked contrite and suddenly capitulated. 'Oh do stop crying. Go and be a damned priest! At least you won't break some poor girl's heart!'


It had not taken long for her words to come true. A year at most. A year which fed his unbelief and his scorn for the clergy until they outstripped hers.

Dan no longer attended confession. He used to be like all the rest, unloading his guilts in routine orgies of self-accusation, leaving the church renewed and free to start the cycle again like a toilet cistern slowly replenishing itself.

He believed in sin and evil, sure enough. What he despised was the unspectacular penances of fastings and ready-made prayers, the petty listings of mortal and venial sins which seemed to concentrate on the top shreds of public behavior. Evil was elusive; it belonged more to the silent half-formed curses, the nameless swift wraths and desires that leak out of everyone in minute betraying gestures. Dan carried with him the sense that everyone was more dangerous than they appeared or realized.

Dan rubbed his eyes and forced himself to read the medical history of the jaundiced mayoress who had spent the last few years awash in vodka. 'I'd have found a better use for your cash, dear,' he thought, enjoying his lack of mercy.

'You're looking sicker than the patients,' the staff nurse scolded him as she bustled in. 'What's wrong with you?'

'I'm a bit worried, that's all.'

'The exams?' she inquired kindly.

'No, no, a shortage of funds. Well, worse than that. I'm in extremis. Thinking of dropping out of the course.'

'You mustn't do that.'

'Whyever not?'

She blushed. 'Everyone thinks so highly of you . . . Why don't you speak to that McGuire. He's engaged to your wife's sister, isn't he? He's famous for knowing the ways and means.'

'Mr Fixit? I won't go to him with my begging bowl!'

'I don't mean ask him for money . . . he might have some ideas. You've nothing to lose by talking to him.'

'Only self-respect,' Dan thought, but he knew she was right. Even if McGuire only let him serve behind the bar, it would buy him more time. After work, he went to the pub and found McGuire sitting before the sinking fire.

'Could I have a word in private?'

'Sure thing,' he boomed affably at Dan, and put his arm round him as he ushered him through to the back room. Dan shivered as he caught McGuire's smell of dampness and sour lemons. How could Katrina bear to let this unwashed nightmare near her?

His host sprawled in an armchair and spread his arms wide. 'What can I do for you?'

'I want your opinion. I'm thinking of jacking in my studies, I'm so desperate short of money. Maybe you could introduce me to somebody who would give me a job?'

'Sure, put the wife out to work! There's no scarcity of females to see to the wee lad.'

'Rosaleen won't hear of leaving him.'

'Aye, well, they're all a bit adhesive to the firstborn. Wait till she has a pair of them!'

'God forbid!'

'I wouldn't depend on *Him*,' McGuire said with a sly leer.

'If you've no suggestions . . .'

'Hold your horses. Drink?'

He selected vodka and poured out two glasses.

'I do have a wee idea. Matter of fact, some friends of mine sometimes have the need of discreet medical attention in a hurry, a question of first aid. I'm sure they wouldn't see a pal go without a few quid.'

'I'm not getting involved with the Provos!'

'Why not? It wouldn't be against your principles. You'd be preserving life. And fattening your wallet, what better arrangement?'

'Shotgun wounds should be treated in hospital at once. I know what that quack Campbell does, patching them up so they can be raced over the border for treatment. How many die on the way?'

'There's worse things than death. The Maze . . . I tell you they won't start queuing up at the Royal to be nabbed by the army. Whether you help them or not. You see, the thing is, Campbell's used up now. The army watches his house. So the situation is vacant. It's a wonder they haven't lit on the idea of using you.'

'That's my good fortune, they never think of me because I don't come from round here.'

'Aye, it's partly that you're an unknown quantity. It's also your middle-class origin.' McGuire almost hissed the phrase.

'God knows what they'd order me to do! Even tell them how to get at injured soldiers lying in hospital, maybe! They've killed men in their beds many a time!'

'Hardly the Marquis of Queensbury rules, eh? Whose side are you on, boyo?'

'My side.'

McGuire guffawed. 'Not bad. Not bad.'

He rose to pour them another glass of vodka. 'Here, this'll make a man out of you.'

He drained his own glass, and poured himself another measure.

'Think it over. It's a beautiful idea. Foolproof. The army thinks you're clean. The boys wouldn't use your house, too many raids. Rosaleen could be kept in the dark. A simple phone call, it's always the wrong number if she answers. You could help the cause, help yourself, and maybe save lives.'

'Save their lives so that they can go on taking others!'

'No one enjoys the slaughtering, but you can't make an omelette without cracking eggs.'

'I never tasted an omelette that justified it!'

'You have a renegade's mouth on you.'

'I'm as loyal an Irishman as you. I never see you risking your skin!'

McGuire waved his hand as if to pacify Dan. 'No offence intended. No doubt you have other ways of picking up a bit of cash, other irons in the fire?'

'Thanks for the drink.' Dan moved to the door.

His head was muzzy. He realized he had eaten nothing all day.

'Hey, if you change your mind . . .'

'I'll let you know.'

'Don't break your word!'

What the hell does that mean? Dan wondered.

No, he would not do it. It would mean getting to know all the wrong faces. The army would put him through a mincer to worm out that kind of information. Or the Provos would do him in to stop him from squealing. He imagined their calm unscrupulous faces. He would be nothing to them but a despicable little payee, a repository of dangerous knowledge.

'Oh Christ!' he groaned at how much he had given himself away to McGuire. After all this time of watching his words in public. That fucker McGuire with his insufferable velvety sneers, that's what had loosened his tongue! Suddenly, Dan felt sick and scared. There was a cold menace in McGuire. 'It's a wonder they haven't lit on the idea of using your services.' What if . . .? Would McGuire be mean enough to suggest it to them?

He remembered the way he had spat the words 'your middle-class origin'. But surely he didn't hate him that much? 'No, he just thinks

I'm a puny intellectual, who doesn't know how to live, that's all. I mismanage everything!'

'You took your time!' Rosaleen complained as soon as he appeared. But he saw her eyes were sore from crying. 'Did you speak to your Director of Studies?'

'No,' he sighed. 'I've done nothing yet.'

Her face lightened. 'If we hang on for a while . . .'

'I hope you've brighter ideas than me,' he said ruefully. 'I went to McGuire. A waste of time . . . Except for him. He enjoyed patronizing.'

'Don't worry about that. He's a person of no consequence.'

He laughed at the sudden deflation of McGuire's Machiavellian image, then broke into a dry tearless sobbing.

'You're so lonely,' Rosaleen said. She came and held him. 'Never mind him. We'll be all right, you'll see . . .'

'I've been bad to you.'

He felt her stiffen and sink away from him.

'Rosaleen, what?'

'Nothing.'

# 5

The man's face at the window made her gasp. She dashed to the door and railed at him: 'Can't you ever leave us alone, nosey? Haven't you had an eyeful?'

Marty Boyle was standing in the street behind the soldier, watching him. She winked at Rosaleen and spoke loudly: 'Whatever do you think it is, Rosaleen?'

'Looks like some of that British government property.'

'Yes, they're not very choosy . . .'

The soldier bridled slightly. The sludge-green uniform made his skin look failed and grey. The eyes were wintery blue.

'Just a routine check, Ma'am.'

'There's a name for men who go gawking at women through windows,' Marty scolded him.

'Fuck off!' he said miserably.

'Did it speak, Rosaleen? Did it utter?'

'The lips definitely moved, Marty.'

He escaped rapidly, his shoulders hunched against their jibes.

'What's all that commotion down the street, Marty?'

'Its just Canadian TV men. They're interviewing Mrs Hartley. You should see her! She's so delighted with herself, she's even taken out her curlers. The Brits ransacked her house during a raid, ripped up floorboards, the lot. She's been keeping the damage intact for four days. The whole Brit press has been given a conducted tour.'

Rosaleen laughed, visualizing the film that would result. An interview with a Brit officer, who would speak with the exquisite enunciation of an ex-Etonian of his men's courtesy and restraint. You would almost believe the Brits got their men in bulk order from monasteries. Then there would be a cut to the havoc in the house, lovingly listed by the aggrieved woman. And all the Prods would watch and say: 'She did it herself. They'll go to any lengths to discredit the army.'

'Come on in, Marty. I'll give you some tea. Why aren't you at school?'

'I took the day off to study. I'm revising Sartre.'

'Sartre! I thought he was taboo.'

'He's on the 'A' level course, so they have no choice. You should see their faces when we read out lines like "We are on a futile journey to the grave".'

'Are we?'

'I don't know. Some of us are on a very quick journey,' Marty said, her eyes darkening.

'Oh, how is your Michael?'

She shrugged. 'Why does everybody link me with him? I was never really going with him.'

'Weren't you?'

'No. Anyway, he just treated me like a spare part. Only interested in becoming a hero. Like all the men round here. You lose them to the prison or the pub, one or the other. Are you happy? With your man and child? The good only earthly Trinity.'

'Flaubert said there is no happiness, only the occasional absence of pain.'

Marty stood up abruptly and went to draw the curtains. 'There! Now there's no danger of anyone spying. The room looks different, doesn't it? We could be anywhere!'

It was true. The shrouded windows made the room so private.

'We'll have the lamp on,' said Rosaleen 'Oh, I know, let's light some candles. We've some left over from Christmas.'

She plundered the sideboard drawers to retrieve the blue and red stumps, all edged and misshapen with teardrops of wax. Soon the room was dotted with tiny centres of candlelight, which, along with the fireglow, seemed to transform the room into a place of mystery and shelter.

Marty sat on the floor hugging her knees, lost in a cocoon of dreamy thoughts. Rosaleen was glad of her presence, no longer wary of the girl's caustic tongue. 'I'm myself now,' she thought.

'Do you ever go downtown, Marty? Maybe we could go sometime?'

'Oh, not for ages. Can't afford to buy any clothes . . . Oh, let's have something to eat, Rosaleen.'

'OK, we could make pancakes, if you like. If I make the mixture, would you cook while I feed Louis?'

68

There was a celebratory air in the kitchen as they bustled around in their preparations. The baby stayed awake but was content enough. When everything was ready Marty carried in the steaming tea and pancakes dripping with butter and honey.

'Oh great,' said Rosaleen. 'It's like Shrove Tuesday.'

'Today is a feast day, February 2nd, remember? Have you not been to Mass, you heathen?'

'Oh yes, it's the Purification. I forgot.'

They concentrated on the food.

Marty spoke first. 'Sometimes I do think about Michael. At the times when I feel hopeless because the fight's gone out of everyone, it makes me wonder what he feels, lying there so tired and filthy still enduring it.'

Rosaleen watched her, saddened by the look on her face. She was like a little old woman huddling by the fire.

One of the candleflames had died. Rosaleen lifted the candle from its holder and stooped over the fire to rekindle the light.

'What will I do?' Marty whispered.

'Oh God, Marty, what will any of us do?'

Marty gave a muffled wail and lurched against Rosaleen, who held her, smoothing back the unruly hair and rocking her gently.

Suddenly Marty shrugged her off. 'For God's sake,' she laughed, 'have you no more hospitable drink than this tea?'

'Don't tell me you've fallen for the booze? And you with a Pioneer pin in your lapel, putting us all to shame!'

'Oh, I only break my vow of temperance in emergencies. So stop stalling and tell me what you've got.'

Rosaleen disappeared into the kitchen where she poured out two inches of whiskey for them both. She lingered there, tidying crockery and folding dish cloths.

'Oh fuss, fuss, stop it,' she told herself. 'You're like someone visiting a friend in hospital. So relieved to get away, so reluctant to go back. Other people's misery is so . . . miserable!' She plucked at some dead leaves on a potted plant, then drained her glass in one swift burning gulp, refilled it and walked briskly back to Marty.

The girls held their glasses and saluted each other solemnly.

'To us,' said Rosaleen.

Marty lowered her eyes. 'To Michael . . . and all of them!'

'Oh yes, yes, of course. To the living dead!' She downed most of the whiskey. 'And the dead. To the freshly despatched! To the long decomposed! May we never stop doing penance for them! . . . You're not drinking your toasts.'

'Rosaleen . . .'

'I *do* know what you should do, Marty. Forget him! Oh, don't look at me like that! He's a different person now anyway. Not even a person. Oh, everyone shies away from talking about it. I mean, really about the way it is. I know they all theorize . . . Imagine it! Naked men skulking in blankets, cooped up in pig sties. Pools of urine and mounds of dung all round them. They're ill, some of them are infested with worms, like corpses already. For what? The right not to wear a prison uniform!'

Marty covered her ears momentarily, then dropped her hands. 'No, no, don't belittle it! It's the principle. They should be regarded as prisoners of war. We are at war, we are a separate people at war. Do you think it's right that when we kill Brits, it's called murder and atrocity, and when they kill us, it's "restoring law and order". Oh, you *know* why. And by the way, I need no assistance from you to imagine Michael's state.'

'OK,' Rosaleen said. 'But he chose his sacrifice. Why does it have to ruin you? You're only seventeen.'

'Choice?' Marty sneered, giving Rosaleen a look loaded with hatred, before sitting down close to the fire. She reached for the sugar bowl and began pressing and moulding the crystals with her thumbs.

'He could be here with you. If he wanted. No one made him join.'

'It's just as well we don't all put our own pleasure first!'

Rosaleen blushed and felt a rush of alarm. 'It's the drink talking, Marty. I'm sorry if I seemed to be insulting Michael or trivializing his beliefs. He is brave and highly principled, no dispute about that.'

'Rosaleen, you were insulting to *me*! You'd think I had no brain the way you were talking to me. Talking down to me.'

'I'm sorry. Forgive it, will you? Blame the demon drink. Oh Marty, you won't quote me? This is a private conversation?'

'Oh, of course. What do you think I am?'

Rosaleen reached out and clasped her hand. 'Friends?'

'Oh, sure.'

They sat together uneasily, staring into the flames. Marty spoke, as if talking to herself. 'I wish Michael and I had "done it" before they got him. Had sex, I mean. Fucked. Whatever is it like? I fancy it must be like a sort of exorcism?'

'The devils soon flock back,' said Rosaleen, examining the hem of her skirt.

'But you're married. Permanent access to relief. Like a glutton let loose in a chocolate factory.'

Marty's voice sounded sly; it did not match her guileless face. What did she guess? Rosaleen wondered. Was she simply trying to wound her in return for her remarks about Michael?

'You'll find out soon enough, if your curiosity is any indication,' she said at last.

Marty frowned. 'But if you possess someone . . .'

'Oh, possession! You know what I'd like? To own myself.'

They heard footsteps crunching up to the outside door, a key turning in the lock.

'God, it's Dan already!'

'The Exorcist,' Marty giggled. 'I'm off.'

'But you don't have to go yet.'

'Oh, I do. I've wasted the entire day talking to you.'

'Thanks. Flattery will get you nowhere.'

'Oh, you know what I mean. I'm supposed to be studying. My mother believes that offering novenas will get me through my exams, but I don't want to rely on it!'

At the front door, Rosaleen restrained her a moment. 'No hard feelings?'

Marty's face turned blithe and broadly smiling. 'Don't look so worried. *Te absolvo*.' She made the sign of the Cross.

'No feelings for me at all perhaps?' Rosaleen wondered as she shut the door, imagining Marty rushing off to denounce her. 'She blasphemed. Against our boys in H-Block.'

H for Hero.

'I'll never drink again,' she vowed.

## 6

He sat suddenly bolt upright in bed. Rosaleen moaned, struggled out and began to grope for the chair. 'My clothes, where . . .?'

'Come back, it's OK.'

'Jesus, I thought it was a raid!'

'What's wrong?' she whispered, climbing back and pressing her chilled flank against him. 'Are you agitating about the money?'

'It was just a dream,' he replied, although it was not a real dream that had disturbed him, but the trudgemill of his day, the quarrel with Rosaleen, McGuire's pink greasy face . . . McGuire! Dan's skin prickled with renewed shame. Somehow he had failed to suggest the distance between them!

'I won't do it!' he thought. 'Is it my fault if they get shot? Nothing will prevent the madmen of the world destroying each other. Those violent acts. Irreversible acts, what were they to do with him? I'll keep out of it, I won't trade with them, and I won't leave . . .'

'Marty's so scared of the Brits marauding through the house, she sleeps in jeans and a sweater. Says she won't be caught in a state of undress!'

'Bastards!' Dan said, clenching his teeth at the thought of Marty, hands on hips, standing up to the soldiers.

'How scornful they are,' he thought, picturing them swooping down the sour alleys like angels of vengeance. It was their regular entertainment to bust in on the sleeping households. Interrupting couplings and snortings, toppling the cheap furniture, laughing at the small indignities of scattered underwear, discarded teeth and spectacles. The people sheltered behind blankets, docile and dreamlocked, too muzzled by shame and surprise to say anything.

How betrayed the children must feel to see their parents so powerless! It reminded him of Rosaleen's reaction the first time she saw her father obey a soldier. During the curfew he was ordered off the street. The great domestic tyrant turned around, meek-faced, and shuffled back inside. Instead of rejoicing at the easy defeat of him, Rosaleen felt cheated and utterly without protection.

'Oh, the Brits are right to despise them,' he thought. ' "Them", I always think "them", never "us". I don't belong here either.' He had never belonged anywhere. He lived friendless as a child with his mother, middle-class Catholics in a prosperous little Protestant town crammed with tradesmen. Now his neighbours and his colleagues both treated him with wariness. Was there no life where he would fit in?

'Oh, I don't care!' he decided. He did not want to be like the other medics. The students were mainly Protestants with mediocre brains but rich parents. So many of the qualified doctors were opportunists building their reputations by feeding off disaster. Like the plastic surgeons who were refining their techniques, refurbishing shattered skulls and faces. Like the psychiatrists who lived in the wine-and-cheese zone writing books about the disturbed children in the ghetto.

'At least I live where the trouble is!' he thought. He could not understand why doctors were such healthy trivial people, so full of ambition. As if they saw nothing. Knew nothing. Had no sense of the fragility of all being. Despite the daily despatches to the morgue. They behaved like complacent lion-tamers who think they hold the beast in permanent thrall. In their own deaths, they would wear the same look of surprise as everybody else. 'No wonder I want to leave! Why should I leave? I'm better than them!' He slammed his fist down on the bed and groaned: 'I won't, won't . . .'

'What? What is it, Dan?'

He leaned away from contact with her.

'Tell me,' she pleaded at him.

'I'm a voyeur of death,' he burst out. 'Here, take my hand, take it. Today it handled a corpse that smelled like bad meat, sweet-tainted bad meat. I can still smell it!'

'I love you for being able to face that . . .'

'My husband the doctor! What will you love me for when I leave?'

'What will you love yourself for if you leave?'

She grasped him by the shoulders and pulled him down. 'It's freezing! Look, everything's more terrible for you because of the money. Once we sort that out . . .'

They lay in silence listening to the rain sluicing the windows.

'I'm wide awake,' she said eventually, touching his arm in a shy way. He sensed her thighs gently parted, breasts tilted towards him. The silent votive offering of access. The panacea. But he did not want that. He was still too full of his vision of the bedroom grapplings in the other houses, the squads of whey-faced children they produced. And he suspected her. She was determined that if he would not confide in her, at least their flesh would have a conversation.

'Rosaleen, you'll tell no one our troubles.'

'Oh, Dan, it's not a crime to be poor.'

'Yes it is. The most unforgivable crime of all. Even worse than being sick.'

'That's a nice thing for a future doctor to say . . .'

He clicked his tongue. 'People are good at shouldering aside their friends who get ill or bereaved or in any kind of trouble. No one wants to be contaminated.'

'That's what my father says: "Never trust anybody." '

'Don't tell your family either. I'll not be answerable to anyone. I'll not depend.'

He reached and held her stiff body as if to soften his words. He pressed his face against her shoulder inhaling her scent with its poignant undertow of skin.

'What will we be like when we're old?' she asked him. He felt it was haunted by another question: 'Will we be together?'

'I suppose it's something you decide.'

'I always seem to do the opposite of what I decide.'

'That puts me in my place,' he thought. 'Major blunder.' But suddenly he felt pity for her. She was scared of herself. The hidden things that seemed to choose her life.

'I don't know how to be old,' he said. 'Maybe I'll be like my mother and refuse to hang around. She would have considered it bad taste.'

'Don't say that.'

'What will we be like then?' he asked.

'You'll be austere. You'll know things. Mysterious things. I'll be . . . Oh, so long as I'm not like other women! So apologetic and invisible!'

'You plan to be a delinquent pensioner, then?' he teased her. 'Hell's granny?'

'Don't! You know what I'm talking about. You can't bear not to be doing something that counts.'

'Do you resent being married?' he inquired coldly.

'No no,' she gave a sigh of tiredness.

After a few moments, he spoke: 'Look, there's no reason why you can't take up that university place in a few years. You'd only be about twenty-five.'

She sat up, furious: 'I don't want some decorative little degree! My head's already full of Woolf and Kafka and Eliot and their beautiful ways of saying: "Life is agony!" I know it's agony. I just don't want to open my legs to it!'

'Don't shout! You don't have to study literature. You were brilliant at so many things.'

'Oh yes. Brilliant at writing essays, brilliant at arguing people into the dust, brilliant at getting magnificent headaches, brilliant at being oversensitive.' She began to weep. 'Oh, why are we so miserable?'

'I don't know.'

He pulled her towards him and rested his head against her shoulder. He did not want to talk any more, to weary himself with any analysis of their joint and separate miseries. He soothed her almost into sleep before he made love to her. Suddenly in the middle of her familiar repertoire of movements she murmured and touched his hair with a tenderness that surprised him and made him at peace.

Dan was walking towards the hospital when a man intercepted him. 'Hey mister, lost all my cash, pickpockets . . .' Smoke-shot eyes, whiskey breath.

Dan removed his pestering hand. 'Away on home!' and watched him lurching on down the street making his boozy entreaties to the shining air. 'That bastard McGuire must have kept his shebeen open till near dawn,' he thought. 'The great patriot! Keeping the whole populace a-swill in cheap stolen liquor! Oh, fuck McGuire!' Why did he keep coming into Dan's mind like some pop-up demon in a children's book? He decided that next time they met he would treat McGuire the way Rosaleen did. With a pained distracted courtesy, while her eyes scanned the company as if she hoped to meet someone more interesting.

He smiled a little to think that he himself could still look like a soft touch. His solid material miseries were not evident, thank God. Every person he passed looked adult and ill, even the children. Almost all living on a diet of booze and Valium sandwiches.

He passed by a yawning soldier at the barricade. 'We mustn't side with them,' he decided. Death-dealers! And the IRA as well and the politicians screaming their dog-eared slogans! It was a question of allegiance. Let them collaborate with death. He was on the side of life.

He reached the ward and saw Mary, the staff nurse, through the office window. She always looked the same. Throttled in the high-necked uniform, beautiful severe face. In her immaculate white dress and silent shoes she could almost seem as bodiless as a visitant, but she ruined the vision by her constant nervous coughing.

'Oh, oh, hello,' she said.

'Hi, how's Mrs Dwyer?'

'She had a restless night. And she's in a right old mood. Wouldn't talk to the priest this morning.'

'I don't blame her,' Dan snapped, thinking of the chaplain's professional courtesies, the way he said, 'Can I help you?' as if he were endlessly available.

'You'd think she'd be grateful for a priest. In the circumstances.'

'Religious faith depends on a functioning carcass!' he said, shutting the door roughly as he went out.

He was glad to see that Mrs Dwyer's husband was not there. That breezy awkward man who brought his wife nothing but social pleasantries! 'The weather's dreadful, you're not missing much . . . Great staff in here, they'll have you on your feet in no time.' It was as if he dare not acknowledge her approaching death, he dare not share it. But it had enraged Dan to see the wretched look in her eyes. The flesh had turned against the person who dwelled within it, and she was not even permitted to speak out! He had gone over to her that first time. 'Are you scared?'

'No, no, I'm all right.'

'No, you're not, you're frightened, you are,' he coaxed her like a lover until she cried and grabbed his hand.

'I'm not ready to die. I thought there would be a sign or something, a discovery . . . I know no more than I knew twenty years ago!'

Since then he had talked to her every day. Even when her husband was there, her eyes would follow Dan. She was already parted from her husband. He bent close over her. She opened her eyes, managed a tight smile.

'There is no God,' she said.

'I know.'

'You're too young to know.'

Mary appeared in the doorway. 'Runcie wants you. We've got a new admission . . . Septic abortion,' she mouthed silently.

'I'm not too young to know,' he thought. Is that what it's for? Was he living his old age by proxy?

'I can't do without this,' he realized. 'This daily dose of the truth.'

The new patient was lying writhing in pain, the gold froth of her hair wild on the pillow. Her skin was a raw red coating, the sheet was saturated with blood. 'Gin and bath routine,' he thought, 'and then she tried to skewer the foetus with something.'

'Pyrexia,' the nurse muttered to the consultant. 'Blood loss and contents.' She lifted the lid from a specimen tray to show the expelled matter.

'Nothing counts except this,' Dan thought. 'Nothing can hurt me. I have never been hurt.'

Runcie drew on a cellophane glove. He entered the woman. Her back arched. She screamed.

'Yes, I do love you,' Dan told her silently. 'I love you. I won't ever leave you.'

## 7

Des was in trouble again. Because Burroughs, in his tireless hunt for dirt, had spotted a speck of grit in the barrel of Des's rifle. 'You could grow potatoes in there!' He struck Des across the face and when he failed to look grateful, Burroughs hit him again and threatened to haul him up in front of the CO.

Burroughs. Wall-eyed git with a face begging for plastic surgery. He really had it in for Des. Must be Des's face. Sneer-lines where other people have laugh lines.

Gerry was tired, dead tired all the time. Sleep was impossible. Always feet on the stairs, doors slamming, voices, piercing bird calls, men snoring. Even when he curled round, knees drawn up to his chest, blankets over his head, still he could not sleep.

Shiner was always teasing him. 'Will I sing you a lullaby?'

At night Gerry could hear the dull thud of blows, the yelps of pain from the interrogation block: 'evensong'.

'Shut up. Oh, for God's sake, shut them up, kill them, anything,' he prayed. He understood torture. It was easy. After the first blow, it was easy. At least those Irish gits could cry out. He would like to get his hands on one of those Papists. Interrogate him. Not about murders and hidden guns. He would ask him what did God do before the Creation? Why did Jesus sound so keen on packing people off to Hell? Like some ice-cold sadist. Did Jesus die for everyone? For Shiner? For Shiner and his rainbow collection of pimples. For his symphony of farts? Was Jesus really betrayed? If it was his destiny to be betrayed, it was someone's destiny to betray him. Didn't he order Judas to do it, and orders are orders, aren't they? 'What thou must do, do quickly.'

Maybe Judas also prayed: 'Take this cup away from me.' Judas. Only man beyond salvation. Damned eternally. For treachery.

Betrayal was so natural. Gerry remembered his mother after his father's death. Even on the day of the funeral, the widow sank her mandibles into the steak Gerry offered her. 'Well perhaps just a little,' she sniffed, postponing her crying bout.

For a while Mother took to gin and carpet slippers. The statutory mourning period. Was it four weeks or five? Then she decided to 'get back into circulation'. It was all henna and support hose and school-girl shiny eyes. Before long there were two pairs of tippity toes on the stairs some nights. Soon marriage was announced. ('But I do under-stand, Mother. It's obviously a vocation.') She had met a man through her rheumatism. A faith-healer with a pink piggy face and gifted fingers which had soon strayed into her non-afflicted parts.

Marcus started to come frequently for meals. And overnight stays. Gerry could not bear his mother's sated wishless look. One morning he found her greasy Dutch cap left lying on the bath-edge. He lifted it and threw it in the bin.

That week he joined his mother and Marcus for an evening meal. Marcus spoke to him in the honeyed voice of a job applicant. 'Do you miss your father?'

'No. I hated him,' Gerry said conversationally.

'Oh!'

'After all, he was hateful.'

His mother stood up, eyes brimming. 'How can you be so disloyal?'

'How can you?' he said, glancing at her betrothed before slamming out of the house.

She came to his room next morning. 'You know I can't manage on my own. I'm only human,' she claimed virtuously.

' "Human kind cannot bear very much reality." Human unkind . . .' Gerry thought. Anyway, old T.S. said that. He would know. He had a mad wife who went around with a page from *The Waste Land* tucked into the brim of her hat. Something of a social embarrassment. 'Maybe I should do that?' Gerry thought. 'A label for my brain. Waste land. Cesspit. Rubbish dump. With "Aim here" written at the top.'

Des. Why was Des always avoiding him? Maybe he was mad that Gerry stayed out of trouble? They used to be in everything together. Chasing girls, reading proscribed books, playing hooky from that dump of a school overrun by mental defectives and psychopaths. And that was only the teachers. That was Des's joke. Maybe Des felt betrayed?

Gerry remembered the night John Paradyze and his gang were waiting at the street corner as he and Des approached. A pack of

GBH addicts who terrorized the district. Gerry wanted to turn back but was ashamed to suggest it. Paradyze stared at them, the small bony lobes of his ears working up and down as he chewed gum. There was no expression on his face. When they reached the group, Paradyze pulled a bayonet and held it pointed at Des's chest. Making no attempt to push the blade out of the way, Des slapped his face. A light contemptuous slap. Then he walked on leisurely as if he had brushed a fly off his coat. Gerry decided then that either Des had nerves of steel or no nerves at all. He had wanted to cultivate the same lack of fear. It was disturbing now to watch Des becoming so twitchy.

Fuck it! Gerry got up from the bed and went into the adjoining hut. He wanted to talk to Des, find out why the thick bastard was getting into trouble all the time.

No one was there. Des's kit was laid out on the bed. Clothes smooth as glass. They looked unworn. Shoes and belt polished to mirror finish.

Cautiously Gerry opened the tiny bedside cupboard. Photographs tumbled out. Des's sister and parents. Des himself in countless poses. In and out of the garden. With and without guitar. With long hair and a skinhead cut. In a black polo neck and smoking a drooping Gauloise. That was his Sartre period, Gerry thought, rummaging through the rest of the things. A packet of condoms (chivalry not yet dead), a novel by Marquez. Surprise surprise, a Bible.

'Find anything?' Des said gently, suddenly appearing.

'Oh no, I . . .'

'Why are you poking through my things?' His voice was bored.

'I don't know. I came looking for you . . .'

Des seemed not to listen. He gathered up the photographs. 'My old man took all of these. Always clicking away he was, recording everything. It's a way of . . . I don't know. Reminding us. This is you. Click. Here you are. Snap . . . know what I mean?'

'My parents never wanted my ugly mug around. In the flesh or out of it.'

'He also collects butterflies and moths. Rows of insects with pins through them.'

'Have you seen the light?' Gerry pointed to the Bible.

'Listen to this.' Des flicked through the pages until he found the place. 'All streams run to the sea, but the sea is not full . . . All things are full of weariness; a man cannot utter it; the eye is not satisfied with

80

seeing, nor the ear filled with hearing . . .'

'Beautiful.'

'Yes. Too fucken beautiful.'

'Des, why don't you play along with Burroughs? Stop giving him excuses.'

There was silence. Gerry wondered if Des heard him. 'But he's looking straight at me.'

'Where would those Irish twats be without their war?' Des asked.

'Well, there would be more of them,' Gerry tried to raise a smile.

'They'd be like us. No point.'

'No point?'

'No vocation. We'll drive ye to the boat. . . . We'll send ye home in boxes . . .' He tried to copy the harsh Belfast speech but his voice faltered as if he would cry.

'Des, don't let them get to you. They hate all of us. It's not personal.'

Des laughed. 'Shut up, moron. I want to be hated for *myself*.'

Silence again. Des spoke first.

'Do you remember that bird I used to go with, Paula, the National Fronter?'

'The dumb brunette?'

'Yes. She used to insist that the Nazis didn't kill six million Jews . . . And she was right. No one died.'

'Oh, so all those photographs of skeletons were a trick?'

Des waved his hand impatiently. 'Listen. The killers made death not count. Extermination in bulk. They made it anonymous. Nothing belonged to those Jews and they belonged to no one. It's as if they never were. They never were.'

'No.'

'Yes.'

'Just because they had no deathbed scenes? No famous last words, gloating relatives, weeping friends?'

'There are light bulb factories in Hiroshima now. Light out of darkness. Commerce rules . . . It'll be the same after this stupid fight. I don't want to be here any more.'

'We could buy ourselves out.'

'We?'

Gerry reddened, but Des was smiling. 'It takes too long.'

He stood up and began to pull on his jacket.

'You not wearing your flak?'

'Makes me sweat.'

'At least it's some protection.' Gerry said.

'Yeah.'

'One of the many perks of the job. Bullet-proof vests, free funerals ...'

Des turned on him. 'Look, you, I am *not* responsible for you joining up!'

Gerry gasped. 'I never said you were!'

'Look after your fucken self, OK?'

# 8

She wheeled the pram along the street, steering her way through rubble. The baby's frail cry went on and on, maddening, persistent. A woman passing by gave Rosaleen a frosty glare as if she were to blame for the child's misery. And perhaps she was. There seemed to be some magical and draining connection between them, so that if she had a sudden fit of tearfulness, it would be answered at once by his bawling even when they were in different rooms. And sometimes he would look at her with a calm judicial gaze as if he guessed her resentment of him. She walked as fast as possible, bored with the familiar streets. Everyone looked so forgotten, except for one or two jaunty hard-faced youths. Leaving the wailing child outside the post office, she went in to collect her family allowance, feeling as meek as a wayward schoolgirl about to be rebuked. The clerk was a Protestant with cunning self-righteous lips. She always counted out the notes and coins with a supernatural slowness which seemed calculated to insult. Rosaleen's father told her that once this clerk had refused to pay a woman who signed her name in Irish. 'You have to be British to get a British handout,' she said. It was hard to believe that she would dare to say that in an area where it was risky for Protestants even to venture. How many people were killed on the basis of malicious stories?

'Here you are, Mrs Keenan.' The clerk passed over the money piece by piece, eyeing Rosaleen with baleful dignity.

Rosaleen shivered at the sight of the grainy warts on the woman's hand and mouthed her thanks, plunging the money quickly into her pocket.

'Why doesn't she get rid of them?' she wondered, unbraking the pram and remembering her own wincing childhood ordeal when she had a crop of warts burnt off with acid in the local hospital. The warts appeared when she was seven, tracking along her knuckles and inside fingers. It was at the time she began to be troubled by religious anxiety. 'God knows your every thought before it even happens,' the priests said. And intention was the same thing as act.

With effort she could control her words and deeds, but not her thoughts. She believed that the humiliating crop of warts was the outward tell-tale sign of her sinful interior life. Especially when charms, spells and beseechings of saints did not remove them.

Once she was playing with a friend in her backyard, some game that included dancing, hands clasped with partner's. The other girl's face puckered with distaste: 'I'm not holding your hand!'

'I don't want you to!' Rosaleen shouted at her. 'I hate you.'

She looked up to see her father framed in the kitchen doorway, watching them. How long had he been there? She could hardly breathe, as she waited for him to bear down on her, slap her, disgrace her in front of Nora. He winked!

Flushed and victorious, she turned to Nora. 'Get out or I'll hit you!' It meant that he loved her, he wanted her to have no friends, he wanted her all to himself!

But later, she sat across the table from him watching with love and dread as he ate in silent concentration. He had the same closed face, no words or smiles for her or anyone. Did she imagine the wink? Did he only squint in the sunlight?

When she reached home, the baby began to cry with renewed vigour while she hurried to prepare him a feed, letting it overheat in her distraction.

'Oh, shut up, will you?' she said, looking in despair at the furious bubbles on the milk's surface. 'It's too hot. Believe me, you really wouldn't appreciate it just yet.' She imagined what would happen if she stuffed it into his noisy mouth. His wise old man's face would turn dark red, the eyes would bulge.

'Oh, stop it, stop it,' she told herself, afraid of her thoughts.

She tested the liquid on her hand before placing the teat into the child's mouth, and then watched his face as he sucked greedily. It was her own face in miniature. His face was assembled from parts of her. Wasn't that enough? Must he always want more and more of her? Strange that his body had battled its way out of hers. She remembered it like a dream. Her bloody chafed thighs, a hard boulder tearing her guts, an elegant censorious doctor scolding her for not pushing. Louis stopped feeding and began to twist his mouth and make tortured little sounds as if straining to speak to her. She loved

84

this cheerful squawking mood. 'I nearly forgot you today,' she chattered. 'Nearly left you outside the post office. What would you have done about that?'

She kissed him as he chuckled and flailed at her with his hands, gently tapping her face.

'Don't you shove me away,' she said laughing, as he kept on pushing at her face. Her eye caught the picture of Jesus on the opposite wall. Dan always ridiculed the picture: 'He looks like someone jerking off,' he said. And she saw it now with the same irreverence: the eyes rolled back in sexual swoon, the mouth set in a little rictus of abandon. Loss of faith was something they shared like fellow-conspirators, for they were unable to talk about it to anyone else. But Dan did not share her sense of being cheated, her terror of emptiness.

She re-read the New Testament in amazement, hating the Jesus she found there. A righteous prig blasting fig-trees, turfing money-lenders out of the temple. And his cruel impossible demands! Thoughts and deeds are the same thing! Love your enemies! Not that he forgave his own opponents. No, they were destined for 'everlasting torment', which he described with gloating malice. And, oh, how he wanted to die! He invited it, insisted. Elected his own betrayer. She felt sorry for Pilate. What else could he have done? She admired his cool sardonic wit in placing that title 'King of the Jews' on Jesus. And now we are all supposed to mourn him, she thought, and be grateful for his 'sacrifice', and do penance. Why should the cross be our greatest emblem of blameless suffering? He wanted to die! What about Aidan? Who did not want, did not deserve, who *should not* have died?

The baby had stopped crowing. With that miraculous suddenness that always surprised Rosaleen, sleep claimed him. 'Oh no, don't go away,' she whispered. But she placed him gently in his cot.

She fingered the silver crucifix around her neck, remembering the time a street-corner Evangelist preacher waylaid her in the city centre. 'Are you washed in the Blood of Lamb?' he pleaded at her, pinning her arms to her sides while he prayed, his rank cheesy breath on her face, his eyes like hard stones. 'Lord, give me the words to touch the heart of this child, to touch her to the very heart.' She stood chill and arrogant, unafraid of such a shabby mirthless clown, then laughed at his sudden flinching expression when he caught sight of the crucifix, which branded her a Catholic. It acted like the shining crosses in Dracula films that make the vampires reel back, shielding their eyes.

She stared at herself in the mirror, her hands automatically moving to cover her stomach. She was afraid of her own body, worried about pregnancy since *that* night. It had been so brutal, such an interruption in her existence. She thought suddenly of Katrina, with her insolent, kittenish looks, the way she clattered around in absurd high heels. 'I'm not like her. You're not like her.'

Katrina was fond of divulging details of her sexual life. The other day she told Rosaleen that McGuire said he loved her orgasms; they were like a 'standing ovation'.

'So, you're just the applause, then?'

'Keeps him happy,' she said peacefully, while Rosaleen saw clearly Katrina's hold on McGuire. It was her mixture of lust and primitive female subservience. Hard-headed and waspish in all her other dealings, but obedient and suitably grateful in bed.

'I am not my body,' Rosaleen thought, and felt the truth of that. She experienced her body as some clownish uncomfortable double of herself. Surely the exterior physical aspect of a person was the least important part? And yet the body could betray you. It had dismayed her that it had not seemed to mind pregnancy at all!

She felt dazed as if some drug was discharging in her veins. With any luck it meant a period was coming. And then she would do something, she *must* do something. She had no qualms any longer about contraception and was scornful of the Church's view of childless marriage as 'mere concubinage'. She had laughed at the tortured logic in *Humanae Vitae* which advocated contraception by the rhythm method, but condemned all other means, allowing the former because it leaves the act of intercourse as 'the kind of act by which life is transmitted'. But how to obtain contraception? Her doctor would not help. She would not ask Katrina. Perhaps that journalist, Naomi? But Rosaleen did not trust Naomi, who was always plundering their lives for her articles, always asking questions that were a blow to pride.

She heard the rattle of the letter-box and ran out to find an envelope on the mat. 'At this time of day?' She opened it and read the words that swam into a sickening blur. 'No, I don't want this. This is a mistake.' What if someone saw him push the note through her door?

Maybe she was already under suspicion and this was a ruse to make her betray herself? For a moment she wanted that. They would stand round her in a circle. Cold eyes and lip-lickings. She would know at last who killed Aidan. 'Murderers,' she would scream at them. But then she would join Aidan. To be consumed by the same worm. The only unity they would ever have. 'No, I don't have to die because you died.' But how could she outfox them? No, no. No one knew. But that soldier! Love at first screw! Nonsense. Dangerous nonsense. There was a knock behind her. She crumpled the letter and opened the door to Katrina.

'Rosaleen, have you seen Leo at all?'

'No, sure he never comes near me. Why?'

'He's been out the entire night, no sign of him.'

'Probably with a girl, you know him.'

'Yes, but the things that happen . . . I won't be happy till I see him walking through the door.'

'I think I'll go round home. Mother's demented, I suppose? That Leo puts years on her.'

Her father sat in the armchair, stroking and clutching at his knees as if to soothe himself. He had run his fingers through his hair, making it stand up in a peak. Rosaleen was afraid at the sight of him, ordinarily so contained and sullen, now harassed and oddly ridiculous.

'I'm sure he'll turn up any minute,' she said lamely, her own worrisome doubts sounding in her voice.

'He's not careful enough,' her mother said. 'You've got to stick to your own these days. And keep a guard on your tongue. Oh, why couldn't I have had all girls?'

'Oh, not again,' Rosaleen prayed, remembering Aidan in his coffin, rosary beads twisted round his joined hands, candlelight flickering over his face, giving it a fake teasing mobility that had made her cry with rage.

'It's one o'clock, Owen,' her mother spoke, indicating the radio.

'Aye, turn it on.'

They sat stiffly listening to the news, waiting for word of unidentified bodies, avoiding each other's eyes.

'God, I hate this country . . .' Rosaleen thought.

There was a sudden crash like the sound of falling furniture in the kitchen. Rosaleen ran out, followed by her mother. Both women halted at the sight of Leo slumped in the doorway, until he started to sob.

'Get some bandages, get Katrina, tell her to get McGuire's car to take him to hospital,' her mother ordered.

When Rosaleen came back with cold compresses, Leo was stretched on the settee. His face, usually so proud and brazen, was swollen with bruises and tears, his trousers hung in tatters over burnt legs. Rosaleen kneeled, breathing in his close panicked odour and placed a cool cloth on the charred skin, making him wince.

'I'm sorry, sorry,' she murmured, turning to stop her tears splashing on to his sores. 'Moral degenerate,' she read uncomprehending. There was a notice pinned to his shirt with 'Moral degenerate' scrawled over it! Rosaleen snatched it away.

Their mother was patting and soothing him: 'My love, my love, who did it to you? Why? Was it Protestants? Where did you go?'

His speech was snarled and ugly, as if his tongue was thickened: 'Tattoo. They said . . . next time.'

'But you know nothing. You've never even been lifted.'

'No,' he jerked his head as if impatient. 'Keep away from bad women.'

He gave a sound that was half giggle, half sob. 'Said I take drugs.'

Suddenly her father loomed over them.

'Everybody!' he shouted in a raw strangled voice. 'Everybody! Everybody's rotten!'

He broke into tears, his face stricken and tender with love, and reached out to hold Leo's head.

Rosaleen fled from the house as soon as possible, unable to bear what she had seen. He loved Leo! Well, she hated him! Leo with his burned legs and battered face! She knew her father would not care if anything happened to *her*.

She remembered how casually he reacted when a man had followed her home from school every day for weeks. 'It's your own fault for tarting yourself up.'

'Maybe you think I should be like Tess of the D'Urbervilles with tied back hair and shaved eyebrows?'

'Tess of the D'Urbervilles! So we all know you read books!'

Dan was waiting when she reached home all out of breath, her hair wrecked.

'What's all the excitement? Where's the kid?'

'With Katrina. It's Leo. Oh, Dan, he's been tortured.'

'Why the hell — ?'

She started to walk up and down, ranting: 'Fooling around with women and drugs. It was our dear "boys". The new priesthood. Taking time off from the war to instil "decency" into my brother!'

'Is Leo all right?'

'Oh, I don't know.'

'Why did you come away, then?'

'Oh, everyone's fussing over him. You should see my father weeping and wailing!'

She looked boldly at Dan and burst out, 'Damn Leo, he *is* a bloody moral degenerate!' then wept with shame, covering her face.

'You're jealous,' Dan said, his voice full of forgiving bitterness. 'You care more for your stupid father than you do for me.'

'No! Do I? You understand, don't you? Your mother . . .'

'I don't care about her!'

'Oh, you do. Everything you do is a kind of quarrel with her. Maybe we could help each other?'

'I don't need that kind of help. The emotions do become less violent in time.'

'As one matures?' she sneered. 'It's easy for you. You've never had any feelings!'

'Oh, you're the great one for feelings. For other people. Like bloody Aidan. You'd rather have a ghost than a real man!'

'Oh, where are you going?'

'Mind your own business. I'm going to McGuire's.'

'Please don't go out, Dan, stay here.'

He clutched her arm. 'Why, what's to tempt me?'

Her body shrank from his touch. She hated the sly grace of him, his swarthy, unknowable face.

He released her and walked out.

'Prefer ghosts, do I?' she muttered to herself. 'I'll get away from you. All of you . . . And live. Live and live . . .'

She brushed her tangled hair with quick familiar skill, and sprayed on scent, remembering Dan's dislike of it: 'Your suffocating shopgirl scent.'

'God, what a mess,' she thought, pausing at the door to look back at the room. 'The lived-in look,' she moaned to herself as she lifted a forgotten cup from the floor, her eye taking in worse chaos. 'Oh, to hell with it! She replaced the cup behind the chair where a scarf of hers lay buried and crumpled beneath a heap of baby clothes. It was an old present from Dan, a wispy scarf bespattered with shining sequins which used to shed themselves as she moved. Little glinting specks littered the carpet now as she handled it. 'Oh damn it. Oh damn you.'

She tried to wrench the scarf in two, then stopped, a sudden sadness flooding out her fury. She stared for a moment at the scarf, its faded glamour, the stains from the baby's smeary fingers. She folded it carefully and placed it in a drawer like some treasured object.

Feeling somehow absolved, she took off her red coat and donned a black one. 'Musn't be a great blob of scarlet. The scarlet woman . . .'


Outside again, in the dank street, her footsteps sounded unnatural, echoing and loud. 'Don't go. Go back. Stop,' she told herself. But she rushed on heedless as if caught up in an action as inevitable as birth. Meeting no one, she entered quickly into the shadowy wind-ripped factory. He was there, his face like a pale moon in the darkness.

She tugged her coat tighter around her, while they looked shyly at each other.

'This is a queer place,' she whispered.

'You came,' he said, looking sheepish and smiling.

'I'm a moral degenerate,' she laughed, cupping her hand over her mouth, afraid of the loudness of her sounds.

'What are you laughing at?'

'Your accent.'

'I'm not too mad about yours either. Is it Belfast?'

'No, Bangladesh.'

He moved closer towards her. 'Well, what do you want?' he asked playfully.

'I don't want anything. I want you to leave me alone. Do you know what they'd do . . .'

'They might do it anyway.'

He reached out and fingered her Crucifix. 'Papist,' he said quietly.

'Rapist! . . . I don't want anything. I'm not used to wanting things.'

'Why not?'

'I don't know. Look, I'd better go. I have to collect my son.'

'I wish we were somewhere else. I wish we could do as we please.'

His face was so eager and wistful and young, she could not look away. She had a sudden impulse to touch his dark springy hair. Hastily, she burrowed her hand up the sleeve of her coat. But his hair was so unlike the other soldiers'. Dull mats pasted to their skulls. Thatch-coloured like their uniforms.

'Do you hate me?'

'I don't know.'

'Don't know much, do you?'

'If someone asks me a question I never know what to say. It's as if I don't exist half the time. Oh, that's crazy, don't listen.'

'No, I know what you mean. It's like being in a foreign country. Not knowing what to do and jumping out of your skin if someone talks to you.'

'You *are* in a foreign country,' she said kindly, then rounded on him: 'Well, nobody invited you!'

They stood gaping at each other like startled enemies. Desire shot through her so that she felt as if her stomach and her legs were dissolving. Her face uptilted, her body swayed.

'Well, I'm here, anyway,' he said finally, straining her against him.

'Come over here,' he said leading her across the perilous shattered floor away from the cold rushes of wind.

She let herself be guided by him until she stumbled against a stone, crying out in surprise.

'Quiet,' he pleaded.

'Oh, my foot,' she moaned.

She had a sudden memory of her neighbour, who was one of the first batch of internees. John McFadden. That unstoppable orator. Always arguing with those who would listen and with those who would not. His ruddy pouched face, tears settling in the creases as he held up his torn feet. 'Look, the fuckers made me walk over a dirty great floor covered with broken glass. Then they took us up in a 'copter, said we were sixty feet high and they were going to drop us out; we'd never be heard from again. Sure, it was only about eight feet off the ground, but we believed them. What class of madmen are they? I'd like to squeeze the very life out of them, so I would . . .'

She glanced at the soldier's profile. 'Murderer,' she thought, pulling him towards her.

'Not here.' He steered her into the sheltered corner of the room.

First she was aware of nothing but the shock of his cold mouth on hers, her struggle for breath as he kissed her. McFadden's face came at her, mean with reproach. 'Go away, I don't care,' she thought. She remembered Katrina's smug after-sex face, the muffled cries and blows that sometimes used to come from her parents' bedroom. 'Meaning passion? Meaning love? No, it can't be so. It must not be so.'

'No!' she said when he began to tug at her jeans. He swore as they stuck at the thigh, and kneeled down to wrench her free of them. She watched his blind intent face as he entered her.

'God, it has nothing to do with me. I could be anyone. I don't care.'

She grabbed him closer and toiled with him, hurtling towards nothingness. When he eased himself gently away from her, she heard her voice say: 'I love you.' The words seemed to echo importantly in the silence.

'Christ, is that all it is?' she thought. 'The body getting what it wants? The dumb thankful body?'

'I love you,' he said.

'Oh fuck off!' She leaned away from him.

'Don't, don't,' he coaxed, stooping to pick up her coat. 'Put this on. You'll catch your death . . .' He looked penitent, as if he wanted to bite back the words. He smoothed his hair, buckled on his belt that was weighted with a shiny holster and revolver. 'Like an extra bloody prick,' she thought.

'How many people have you killed?'

'None!'

'You're just an apprentice, then.'

'You wouldn't be afraid of me if you really knew me. What's so funny about that?'

'People are even more frightening when you know them.'

'Sometimes I dream about finding the man who killed Mark. My mate. I'd like to finish *him* off. I'd want him to know why, though. I'd say: "This is what you did, and now I'm doing it to you." '

'I wouldn't bother with explanations,' she said, thinking of Aidan. 'They didn't even give him a chance to pray.'

'Listen,' he said. 'I have to go.'

'Oh, go on then!' She swerved to avoid his arms.

'When will you see me again?'

'Again?'

92

'You know that scrubland near the barracks? No one ever goes there. It's too near us.'

'All right, I'll try, but send me no more notes. You mustn't do that.'

'When will you come?'

She tried to remember Dan's working times. 'Oh, what will I do?' she wailed, burying her head on his shoulder, and then in a brisk matter-of-fact voice: 'Wednesday. After dark. If I can.'

'You must go now. I'll watch you out of sight, then I'll go down the back lane.'

'What's your name?'

'Gerry.'

'Suppose you'll brag to the other foreigners about treating yourself to one of the natives.'

He said nothing, only kept his eyes on hers for a long moment. They peered out of the broken window. 'Right. Go now.'

She walked quickly homewards, trying to breathe evenly. At the end of the street she paused to calm herself, looking down at the black mill pond, inhaling the city smells of age and dirt. There was a lone swan gliding near the far bank.

'She can fly away anytime,' Rosaleen thought.

# 9

'Gerry? Are you there? Are you hiding?' She awoke suddenly, blinking at the shadows in the room. Gerry! Had she said something? Spoken aloud? Dan did not stir. Even in sleep, he was frowning, his face beautiful and grave, one arm shielding his chest.

Wednesday. The day she had promised to meet Gerry. 'Promise! I never promised a thing!' Let him wait. Let him despair if he wanted. 'Am I supposed to risk my life? For you?' As she rose she tugged on her icy dressing gown and became aware of an ache in her body. Was it . . .? The period was so late. She hesitated, praying, willing the menstrual flow, then pressed her hand between her legs, withdrawing it smeared with blood. She ran out of the room and downstairs, her whole body light and swift with the astonishment of relief.

It was a reprieve. A sign. She could have a new life, scoured clean of everything that had happened.

But Gerry . . . Would he allow her? 'Oh, go away, die, disappear.' His hangdog face, his hovering at corners like the incarnation of her own guilt! She knew she must finally renage on Gerry, renounce him utterly.

There was still no sound of Dan stirring. Kneeling by the hearth, Rosaleen made the act of contrition, mouthing the words she knew by heart: 'O my God, I am sorry and beg pardon for all my sins and detest them above all things, because they deserve your dreadful punishments, because they have crucified my loving Saviour Jesus Christ, and, most of all, because they offend your infinite goodness; and I firmly resolve, by the help of your grace, never to offend you again, and carefully to avoid the occasions of sin.'

'Avoid occasions of sin,' she thought. Yes, it was as simple as that.

Dan appeared eventually, looking sore-eyed as if he had not slept. 'You don't look well.'

'Nor do you. I can't find anything. My toothbrush. Keys.'

'My period's started, that's why. I'm all right, really.'

'Oh good.' He sighed. 'I'll make some tea.'

'Have you the time?'

'No, but I want some. Tea tastes better when you're having your period! I'm sorry,' he laughed, 'it's just that I thought you were pregnant. You seemed so "couldn't care less" lately, and it made me think . . . well . . . I'm glad you're not pregnant.' He kneeled down to address his congratulations to her reproductive system: 'Thank you, merciful ovaries, Fallopians, ovum . . .'

'Sperm! Don't forget to thank them for their failure!'

'No, it's dangerous to provoke them!'

He stopped fooling around. 'I wish I could act as freely as I think. I mean, it would be disastrous to have another child. And yet, we risk it. Such a good young Catholic couple.'

He made her feel ashamed. 'Maybe that's not why we . . . Catholicism might have nothing to do with it.'

'It wouldn't be so bad if those priests weren't absolutely thick. I hate them. What do they know about anything? Sex-shy clowns. Comforting themselves with big meals and cigars and liqueurs. Those stupid faces. All red with imminent cardiacs and, oh, you know that look? Sort of subdued indeterminate wrath as if they see sin everywhere.'

'You know the official line. It's the office, not the man that counts . . .'

'No! If there was really any miracle in the Mass, if a human man was the channel for the Holy Spirit, he would be touched by it, transformed, wouldn't he? He wouldn't go round grumbling about the weather, sucking his teeth, yawning in the confessional . . .'

'Will you get some contraceptives?' she said almost angrily. She did not like to have to play the voice of practical wisdom while he was sorting through his metaphysics.

'They smell like rubber gloves.'

'Oh Jesus, Dan!'

'Would it bother you?'

'The smell or the eternal damnation?'

'Right, I'll get them. I'll get them. A huge hoard. Brothel-loads.'

'You see, you do think there's something bad about it.'

'Sorry. I'm a defrocked priest, remember.'

'That's why you hate priests,' she laughed. 'The unflattering self-recognition.'

They embraced. 'It's settled, then?' she asked him.

'Settled. I like that word. It's my bourgeois soul. Settled stomachs. Settled debts. Oh Christ, I had forgotten about those . . .'

'Dan, won't you think about me working? Possibly working? You were in a bad mood when we talked about it before.'

'Oh, Rosaleen, there is no work. Twenty-one per cent unemployment.'

'I know the statistics. I might manage not to be a statistic.'

'I don't know. Oh, I'd better get a move on.'

'OK. I love you.'

'You haven't said that for ages. I feel bad when you don't say it. Shouldn't tell you that.'

'Official secret?'

He grinned and went to get ready and make the promised tea. After he left for the hospital she worked through the uphill part of the morning, her mood turning dark.

When he was nice to her, her betrayal of him seemed even worse. Besides, five minutes of peace and joy couldn't wipe out their problems. 'Love on the Dole.' She had always been sceptical about that title. Love requires a reasonable income.

She took a sheet of blank paper and wrote down a list of solutions and practical objections as they occurred to her.

Work at home: Low paid and not much available.
Leave Louis with mother: Dan objects.
Leave Louis with childminder: Expensive. I object!
Find employer with crèche: There are none.
Work at night while Dan looks after Louis.

The last idea seemed best. The baby was not so uproarious at night. Dan could study. But what on earth kind of job could she do? She made a mournful recital of her GCE passes: Latin, Irish, French, Classical Greek, Religious Knowledge, Irish History, English Composition, Home Economics . . . Her education was designed to fit her for motherhood, nationalism, and eternity! She had no experience to offer, unless her care of the child and her young brothers and sisters counted. But domestic skills were not her forte. And if she were confined to night work the opportunities narrowed even more.

A waitress? Fawning and flirting for tips. Barwork would be worse, she decided, remembering Katrina, presiding goddess of McGuire's bar. Her exactly calculated exposure of bosom . . . I could always be an auxiliary nurse on permanent night shifts.

But the hospital was Dan's domain. Anyway, she did not know if she could cope with laying out, with disposing of the potted faeces of strangers, witnessing the lonely degradation of the ill every night.

She found the previous day's papers and made a listless inspection of the jobs column, her despondency growing with every repetition of 'Experience essential', 'Typing desirable'. She guessed from the areas mentioned that most of the firms were Protestant. Her religion was a disqualification before she even counted her other disadvantages. 'God, there must be something. I've got to find something.'

How she hated her days! Nothing but a keeping at bay of wet laundry and potato peelings. Even the thought of pen-pushing her way through office hours was glamorous to her.

Oh, why do you want to work? All the workers she knew moaned at the servitude of it. To while away your life? Wile away?

In the second paper, she found this advertisement: Playgroup Assistant. Unity Flats area. Full or part time. National Nursery Examination Board qualification preferred.

Full or part time, she re-read. NNEB preferred. But not necessary. Means they're having trouble finding someone.

No wonder, with that location. Ruined towerblocks near the Protestant Shankill Road. One of the worst flashpoints in the city. A decaying rabbit warren with a rudimentary playground for the kids . . . Not so praiseworthy when the high roofs were a playground for snipers. 'Maybe it's safe enough in daytime. Maybe I could bring Louis with me? No, not a good idea. Anyway, you'll never get it!'

Thankful that she had not yet asked for the phone to be disconnected, she tried to compose herself before dialling but was breathless when she had to speak. 'Are you in work at the moment?'

'No, no, I'm afraid I've never had a job.'

'You could start right away then. Have you just finished college?'

'No, I have 'A' levels, but no further training or qualifications. Due to family commitments.' She felt a wave of blood rush to her face.

The voice remained friendly and neutral. 'Could you come for an interview tomorrow? Say at two forty-five . . . Good. Ask for Thomas Gifford.'

What would she wear? What could she say? The man would think she was presumptuous. She would see it in his face.

What does it matter? she thought. All the worry would be in the anticipation. All the injured pride in the aftermath. During the interview itself, she would scarcely feel at all. Did everyone live the same benumbed life? Is that what Gerry was for? To break the spell? Oh Gerry . . . forget Gerry!

She switched on BBC Radio to distract her mind with some bland good cheer. Terry Wogan was on. Irishman, export variety. Opium for the Missus. Chatting up some embarrassing phone-in contestant who failed to answer the questions in an appallingly facile little competition. Before consigning the poor loser back to lifelong anonymity, Terry flirted with her: 'Are you married, affianced, promised, or just hoping?'

Rosaleen switched off.

What if you were married and still hoping? And couldn't even say what you were hoping for?

About ten minutes later, there was a sharp rap at the window. Marty's face was peering in. She smiled and beckoned to Rosaleen to admit her.

'Are you off school today again?' Rosaleen laughed.

'Going to school interferes with my studies.'

Marty spilled the contents of her bag on to the table, a hoard of cosmetic pots and jars. 'I want you to keep these things for me.'

Rosaleen was already examining the glossy lipsticks and eye-shadows. 'Why?'

'They're nicked. My ma would belt me if she found them, and sure, there's no hiding anything in my house.'

'Where did you get them?'

'The Beauty Playground. Crammed full of assistants it was! I just kept grabbing whatever I fancied and not one of them lifted a finger . . . or a perfectly plucked eyebrow . . .'

While speaking, she began to apply the make-up without restraint or expertise, ending with sprinklings of golden glitter in her hair.

'That's what they wear in the discos over in London,' she declared, swivelling her hips and pouting her plastered mouth.

Rosaleen streaked her own hair with the glitter, then inspected herself and Marty in the mirror. They looked like angelic harlots.

'Are you coming out for a walk?'

'Everybody would stare at us.'

'They do, anyway.'

'There's nowhere to walk. Nowhere exactly picturesque.'

'Yes there is. Up the Black Mountain.'

'It's dangerous.'

'Oh, it's dangerous everywhere! I want to get away from here. Sing at the top of my voice. I've got the loan of O'Casey's alsatian. Come and look at this for a view!'

Rosaleen was steered into the street, where she shielded her eyes to look up at the mountain slopes. She raised her gaze from the sprawling hillside cemetery upwards to the shimmering peak. The sunlight which seemed to lure her to the mountain made the dusty street more oppressive than usual.

'You win. If my mother's in for looking after the kid, I'll call for you in an hour or so.'


Her mother was staring into the sink; she seemed not to listen to Rosaleen's prattle about the job.

'What's wrong?' Rosaleen asked.

'Leo's leaving us. Going to England. He's done nothing only mope round the house since he took that beating. And that woman is urging him on, pledging to follow after. Anything to get rid of him, and save her own precious hide.'

'Isn't it for the best? I mean, he'll be safe there, he'll forget her.'

'And what will he do in England, may I ask?'

'More than he can do here.'

'You don't care if he goes away. Your own flesh and blood.'

'Oh God, Mother, I'd rather never see him and be able to think of him walking free in some other place. Anything must be better than skulking here afraid of being injured by maniacs who think it's their business who he fucks!'

'Don't use language in this house! You should know how a mother feels . . . What is all this about you looking for a job?'

'We're so broke. Anyway, I want a job.'

'What does Dan think about it?'

'The lord and master? He doesn't take it seriously.'

'Which eggs you on like nobody's business, of course. Look at the cut of you for going to an interview. Look at your shoes. Give them to me! You know what I always say: "If you look poor, you'll get poorer." '

'Yes, I know what you always say.'

'You wee bitch.'

Her mother applied polish to the battered shoes and rubbed vigorously at them.

'Oh, it's no use,' she decided. 'Look, Rosaleen, buy a new pair. Here's some money, take it.'

'No, I can't do that. I'd only have to spend it on other things we need.'

'It's for you. You're not to stint yourself.'

'But you do. You're doing it now.'

'I don't want you to have to do things I do. That's why . . .'

'Yes, yes, you told me I didn't have to marry. It was my choice. I believe that's the word.'

'Oh, Rosaleen, dear . . .'

She accepted the money, enclosing it in her palm, and gave her mother a quick hug. She rushed out of the room, afraid she would cry. She ran upstairs to see Leo.


Leo was leaning against the pillows, his face still bruised and important looking.

'You're leaving so?'

'That's it!' he said, sweeping crumbs from his blankets. 'Well, are you going to lecture me about moving to the enemy camp?'

'With friends like the ones who did that to you . . .?'

He gave a smile that vanished at once.

'Will you fly? I think it must be nice to fly.'

'I'm going by boat. I want to feel every inch of the distance.'

'Will she . . .? Is it true that lady is joining you?'

He almost jumped at her question. 'No. I hate her.'

Rosaleen looked away. She wanted to touch him, to say: 'We are the same, you and I.' To tell him he was right to walk away from that shallow insipid life, to tell him . . . to confess.

'Why have you got that glitter stuff in your hair?' he demanded brusquely. 'What's it for, eh?'

She told him about Marty's plundering in the Beauty Playground, how she had filled her voluminous pockets with cosmetics while the sales assistants stood around looking like inflatable dolls. He did not laugh.

'You think you're morally superior, don't you?'

'No! I *know* I'm not. In fact . . .'

'I know you're not, though you always acted high and mighty. I remember you stealing birds' eggs, while the blackbird hopped about like a mad thing.'

'I was only five. I thought they were ornaments.' She wanted to cry. He was like every man she had ever known. Old Testament face. Grievances cherished from the long dead past.

'She's the same,' he muttered. 'God, they half murdered me as if I was some spoiler of innocence! I'm eighteen. She's forty-three. Fuck her! All that silky crossing and uncrossing of legs. You're blushing. Know what I mean, don't you?'

'Don't hate her, Leo.'

'You know what she said to me the first time?' He spoke in a sultry voice: 'I thought you'd never take the hint.'

'You agree with your attackers, then? You just think they punished the wrong person?'

They fell silent for some moments, Rosaleen full of consternation at the thought of having almost told him about Gerry. But Leo looked so fierce and lonely, she did not want to go away. He sighed: 'I don't really want her to be punished. It's just galling to be told all your life to "be a man", then get mauled for not behaving like a eunuch.'

She gave him a mocking sympathetic look. 'But you haven't snuffed anybody out yet. You can't possibly be considered one hundred per cent virile.'

'I haven't been snuffed out either, thank God. I don't want to make a manly corpse for Mother Ireland. Or for any mother figure. I wonder if she knows I'm going away?'

'She couldn't come to see you, Leo, no matter how much she wanted,' Rosaleen said, thinking how Gerry would wait uselessly for her tonight. How long would he linger there?

'I've been thinking all kinds of things cooped up in here. I sometimes wonder if she put them on to me. Maybe she thought I was getting too adhesive. There are days when I think she only let me make love to her by way of apology. Because I saw her so drunk most of the time.'

'What did she say to you? When you were lovers?'

101

'Oh, she loved me, darling,' he said in a coquettish voice.

'People don't know why they make love. With one person rather than another. Do they?'

'Drinkers lie. They tell terrible lies. So that they can keep on drinking.'

'They say drink makes you betray yourself. It makes you speak the truth.'

'People say a lot of things.' Leo gave her a tired bitter look.

'Yes, don't they? Maybe that's why your friend is such an escape-artist. To stop listening to all their cant and speechifying? How else to survive round here?'

'How do *you* escape, Rosie?'

'Same way as you.'

'Sex! Oh, that's nice for Daniel.'

His face looked suddenly closed and reproving, as if she had committed some trespass. So, it was impossible to tell him. Well, she did not like to think of his private body either, and the loving or loveless use of it by some stranger.

'Oh, it's nice for all concerned.'

'You make it sound as if you have a whole troop of victims.'

'Wishful thinking. Would you like a cup of tea?'

He laughed. 'When you lived here, you would never make me a cup of tea!'

'I did so.'

'Not without inviting me to choke on it.'

'You were always so lordly, ordering me about! If you don't like your instructions about "being a man", I don't like mine about how to be a woman!'

'I'd rather be expected to learn how to make tea and cakes than petrol bombs!'

They glared at each other like the practised enemies they were. But the thought of Leo going alone to the boat made Rosaleen relent. She imagined him waiting on deck, the doleful blasts of the foghorn that would toll his farewell.

'Maybe I'll go with you to the harbour?'

'Would you do that?'

'If you want.'

'Are you all right? Are you happy with Daniel?'

'He's a good person.'

102

She stood to go. 'I wish you such luck,' she said with grave formality, and stooped to kiss him but took his hand instead.

Marty's mother answered the door and Rosaleen found herself ushered inside and installed in an armchair in their shadowy front room.

'You'll have a cup of tea?'

'Is Marty ready? I don't think we have time.'

'She must be upstairs. I'll give her a shout.' She paused in the doorway, peering at Rosaleen with fat shining eyes. 'Did you hear about that girl took the overdose? She goes to St Dominic's, same class as our Nuala?'

'No, I didn't hear,' Rosaleen lied.

'They say it'll be a miracle if she lives.' She disappeared, leaving Rosaleen alone with Marty's grandfather, who had not acknowledged or even seemed to notice her presence.

'Miracle if they let any of us live!' he muttered. 'We'll not be leaving it up to miracles!' The old man had been burnt out of his home in the '69 riots and now lived in a state of monomania, convinced the street might be set ablaze at any moment.

'Do you think it will ever end?' She faltered, embarrassed at talking about the strife as if it were a dose of bad weather.

The man turned his sad appraising glance on her. There were grooves of misery tracking his cheeks, his eyes were a pale hazy blue like Marty's. She was so like him, Rosaleen thought, except that Marty had the haughty sullen look which unhappiness gives to the young.

'I'd love to be out there with the best of them. This time it will end! We were the lads would have finished it in '21. Betrayed! After all we did, sacrificed. I filled in every murdering Black and Tan crossed my path. Scum of the earth they were! Set loose out of English jails to come slaying and looting over here.'

'Now they round them up out of dole queues.'

'Not at all! There's no compulsion to earn a living in such a dishonourable way!'

'No. You're right.'

'Hah!'

'How long must we endure this, though?' she burst out. 'You thought you'd finish it in 1921! We've just had another decade of it and the chorus is the same: this is it, end in sight, the big push, the last gasp . . . How much longer?'

'As long as it takes. It's for you, you impudent female person, that good men are laying down their lives.'

'I don't require it, I assure you.'

'It's not for you to say what's required, all the size of you. Attend to your school books.'

'I've left school. I'm a married woman,' she said with dignity.

'He doesn't keep you in line!' He laughed himself into a fit of coughing.

Marty's mother reappeared carrying a trayload of cups. She winked at Rosaleen. 'Has he been bragging about his civil war shenanigans again? Every dog has his day.'

'Mind your own business, you!' he scolded her. 'No one was addressing yourself.'

He turned away to his sad self-communion. Rosaleen watched him as he gulped the tea down his skinny throat. She knew that he was only tolerated in his home. He was glad that she had spoken to him. No wonder he hankered for his fighting days. This is what Leo means, she thought. Fighting is the only way for men to count. How good it was that Leo saw through it. And Dan . . .

Marty entered the room at last, her face scrubbed clean of the cosmetics, leaving her skin flat and pallid. She patted her duffle bag. 'I've got some refreshments for us.'

'Do we need . . .?'

'There are no olde tea shoppes up there.'

Her mother looked up, alert and suspicious. 'Just where are you pair off to?'

'For a stroll.'

'Marty, you'd better tell me where you're going. This is not Bognor Regis.'

'We're running away. I'll send you a postcard . . .'

'Marty,' she reached out to detain her.

'Don't quiz me.'

'I am not quizzing you.'

'You never let me do anything.'

The woman let go of Marty's arm and gave Rosaleen a look of pleading. 'Is it my fault she has no life? Does she think my existence is one round of pleasure? You're a sensible girl, Rosaleen . . .'

'She won't tell you either,' said Marty.

'Aw, get out of my sight, the both of you!'

They waited at the main road for the People's taxi. 'Keep the hound out of sight in case the man drives past us,' Marty urged.

'How the hell do you hide an alsatian?'

'Just act as if he has no connection with us.'

The taxi appeared after an interminable time and they waved it down.

'Mister, would you take us as far as the foot of the hills? We'll pay for the dog.'

'Aye, all right. I'll risk it through Whiterock if you will!'

They were both out of breath as they trudged up the hill.

'You're very like your grandfather,' Rosaleen said, adding quickly, 'facially, I mean.'

'I hate it when people say that! I wonder if I'll go off my head?'

'Of course not. He's an old man. Anyway, he doesn't seem any madder than most people.'

'You don't have to put up with him! He's our skeleton in the cupboard. I get sick of listening to his rantings. He even shouts in his sleep. Dreams he's being chased and put to death.'

'He put down a few himself, by his own account?'

'Not as many as he claims. He multiplies it by his age! But yes, yes, he did. Why else would he dream about it?'

Marty began to sing the reverential ballads of Ireland's past. Rosaleen did not like her voice but she was glad of the singing, which helped to dispel something fearful in the stillness of the air.

After a while, it was calming to be surrounded by farm landscape that had been dug up, sown, reshaped by men's hands. Rosaleen walked in silence, enjoying the fragrant dampness of the earth, the sight of the sky threading itself through the newly leafed trees. 'That would just suit me,' she thought, eyeing one of the ordinary little cottages which dotted the hillside, when Marty stopped her song abruptly.

'This is Hightown Road,' she spoke softly. 'Where Paddy Wilson was killed with his girlfriend. What's her name who used to be on "Come Dancing"?'

'Irene. Her name was Irene.'

Rosaleen shivered. This was the place where they came to talk and be alone. Where they were hacked to pieces.

'When lovers die at the same time, do their souls stay together?' asked Rosaleen.

'Not in their case. She was a Protestant.'

'Marty, do you think you could ever love a Protestant? Or an Englishman?'

'No.'

'Why?'

'Romeo and Juliet?' Marty said sarcastically. 'It would mean hating myself. Spitting on every belief. Betraying everyone.'

Rosaleen stopped and looked back at the bare grey road, the primroses in the hedgerows. 'It looks so normal here, so pleasant. There's no trace.'

Marty shrugged. 'Why should there be? The world doesn't care about us.'

'What about Buchenwald? Auschwitz?'

'What about them?'

'No grass grows there. No flowers. No birds will go there.'

'Loads of gross Germans go. With packed lunches and cameras.'

'People desecrate everything. The earth. Each other. The words they use.'

About a mile further on, Rosaleen began to feel weary. She was sweating. 'Marty, let's stop for a while. We can look down on the city.'

'Good, I like looking down on things,' Marty joked.

They found a sheltered spot in a roadside field and shed their jackets thankfully.

'Doesn't the world look great when you feel out of it? Belfast is a little place. Look at those tiny people . . . I don't believe in God.'

'SShh,' said Marty. 'He'll hear you.'

She lay down with her eyes closed. Rosaleen watched her: the resolute mouth looked so poignant set in the small mould of her features. The faint tattoo of acne, the heavy hair that was redolent of kitchen smells, and yet beautiful. Auburn. Rosaleen pulled some leaves and twined their stems through Marty's hair, making her look like a ruined lovely child.

Marty opened one eye. 'I nearly forgot the picnic!' She sat up and delved into her bag, brought out sandwiches, chocolate cake, and a bottle of vodka which she handed to Rosaleen.

'Here, you, suck on this.'

'Oh no, I will not. It's enough to get out of town. I don't need to be drunk as well.'

'I must say you're great fun!'

'I can't drink. I have an interview tomorrow. Forgot to tell you.'

'Not for a job! What job?'

'Playgroup assistant at Unity Flats.'

Marty's whole face twitched with aversion. Her voice was cold when she spoke finally: 'Oh well, you'll have a boss. Be told what to do all day. That's salvation for some people.'

'It's financial salvation I'm after.'

'I suppose everybody's some kind of whore.'

'What do you mean! Why are you so nasty about it?'

A whore! Rosaleen felt sick suddenly. She could not focus her eyes properly. What did she mean? What did she know?

'You'll be in the pay of a bunch of Unionists. The City Fathers.'

'Oh yes, yes. But it won't serve them. We should claim our fair share of those kind of facilities, and be glad to run them ourselves. It benefits our people.'

'No, it does not. How can you even talk about fair shares? The whole system is built on unfairness! You'll be helping to prolong that rotten discredited system. Look, you know what those flats are like. It's unbearable to live there. So let the people not bear it! Do nothing to mitigate the awfulness of it!'

'What do you think we should do?'

'Concentrate on the war. Get the Brits out. I don't care how much is destroyed in the process. My attitude is: We've never had anything. So let no one have anything!'

Cake crumbs were clinging to Marty's underlip. Rosaleen tried to laugh: 'You want to see the whole city alight just to soothe your nerves?'

'No, to wreck *their* nerves. Proddie nerves and English nerves.'

'How will I take you seriously? Tell me what you do to destroy the system? Do you act as a decoy? Deliver bombs? Rob banks?'

'One does what one can,' she said with self-conscious mystery.

Rosaleen lost her temper. 'Oh, one does what one can! You sound like bloody Princess Anne. You think I'll be selling myself by working for a Unionist council. But you're not free either. You think what you're told to think. Everything you say is an echo of Michael . . . Oh, I'm sorry. Forgive me.'

'It's all right. He's not some unmentionable obscenity. Even if he is living in his own shit. Do I still sound like Princess Anne?'

'I have no noble motives for wanting that job, that's the truth. I need money, and I can't wait for the establishment of the workers' republic to get it. There are other reasons as well.'

'What other reasons?'

'Oh, I should help Dan. I'm not much use to him.'

'Does he think you're not much use?'

'He deserves someone like you. You're so true to Michael.'

'No, I'm not. I used to feel bad if I even laughed at a joke. Or forgot him for a few minutes. Or enjoyed a good meal. Now I don't care any more. Can't do his suffering for him, can I? Don't you think I look different. I'm no longer virgo intacta.'

'Oh, who is he? Anyone I know?'

'Unlikely. It was on a train. From Dublin to Belfast. He had chewed nails. And he was nearly bald, except for two stripes of hair across his skull. It happened in the toilet.'

'In the convenience?' Rosaleen sneered.

Marty rounded on her. 'Do you know you're even getting to *look* like a married woman! Things happen on trains, you know. It's the sense of being nowhere in particular. Being no one in particular.'

'Marty, that's not a reason. Why did you do that?'

'I wanted to "desecrate" my body. People desecrate everything, don't they, nasty creatures?'

'Did you want to abuse your body to match Michael's?'

'What does it matter why I did it?'

'You said that on the train you felt like no one in particular.'

'So what?'

'Maybe that was a good impulse. Maybe you're sick of the claims on you. You want to have possibilities. Start from scratch.'

'Buy me a season ticket.'

'No. A one-way ticket. To nowhere in particular!'

Marty grinned. 'Sounds autobiographical, if you really want to know. I'm sick of this yapping. Pax?'

'Pax.'

## 10

Dan stood in the doorway eyeing McGuire as he leaned laughing over the counter of the bar. Flaccid little body. Surprisingly dainty hands and feet, tiny threads of blood in his eyes. Such a harmless hedonist he looked as he told his usual anecdotes, about the triumphs of the cowardly over the brave, the cunning over the noble, brawn over brain.

Dan felt in his pocket and touched the package to rekindle his wrath. Why could he hold on to no feeling for any length of time?

'Hey Danny,' yelled McGuire, 'come on over, swell the numbers! What'll you have, Doc?' he asked as he fondled Dan's shoulders and coat buttons, gilding his conversation with stunning compliments.

Dan remembered suddenly how he once believed that hypocrisy made everything more bearable and pleasant, how he used to scold Rosaleen for her abrasive manner. 'I need a word with you in private.'

'Again! People will begin to wonder about us, dearie,' said McGuire, performing an exaggerated mincing walk. 'Look, I'm desperate busy, man. This is the lunch time. Have a heart.' The oily film over McGuire's eyes gave him a weak beseeching look.

'Can't wait.' Dan pushed his way through into the back room, McGuire trotting behind him.

'Well, what is it this time?'

Dan took the package from his pocket and tipped the thick wad of yellowing banknotes on to the table. The two men watched each other for a moment.

'Won the pools or something? Where did you get it from?'

'Hardly from an impeccable source.'

'Oh?'

'I want *you* to tell me where I got it from! Or no, I don't want any names. Just return it to whichever murderer or other celebrity of your acquaintance posted it through my door.'

'Look, son, you've got the wrong idea. The wrong idea entirely. I never breathed a word to them. I was only joking that night. Holy God, you don't seriously think . . .'

'So how did they get the idea? Telepathy!'

'Why point the finger at me? You've been whining all over the place about your debts. You've brought this on yourself.'

'You put them on to me. Now you can give them back the cash.'

McGuire lifted the money and began to flick through it.

'You won't find any clues. No donor's signature.'

'J. B. Page. Chief Cashier. Bank of England. That's the only signature you need. Here.' He held out the money to Dan.

'I won't be used by them!'

'You can't be "used" by the 'RA. You're *in* the 'RA. Like all of us.'

'I stand in no line!'

'You'll be top of the queue for a bullet in the head, if you don't wise up!'

'Shut up!' Dan shouted at him, looking wildly round the room, as if it was some place he had run inside for safety, that was not good enough, that was not going to help him.

Katrina's cackling laughter reached him from the outer room. He looked at McGuire. Lobster red face. Indestructible smile. How he hated both of them! Their endless downing of whiskey, their fawning and grinning, their well-advertised pleasuring of each other!

'Look, son, calm down,' McGuire went on. 'A while ago you were complaining because you had no money, now you're complaining because you have plenty. Where's the sense?'

Dan reached out and grabbed at McGuire's lower lip and twisted it, while his other hand gripped the fleshy nose. 'You fucken bloated bedbug! That slut Katrina . . .'

Dan's strength drained away as he looked closely into his opponent's face, at the slow dirty tear curling down his cheek. Two grown men. Such clownish grappling . . . How stupid. How base . . .

His hands dropped to his sides.

'You leave my Katrina out of it. The loveliest thing that ever happened in a man's life . . . God, you try to help people, try to give them some advice, where does it get you? . . .'

Dan thrust the money into his pocket and turned to go.

'I was never fond of you!' McGuire hurled after him.

Outside, some of the houses were already lit against the grey

110

afternoon. Dan walked quickly, feeling visible and vulnerable. Remembering his words, he winced with shame: 'I stand in no line.'

What was he now but a purchased slave? Compared to him, the Provo volunteers were heroes.

But no, Dan knew they were unfree. Weren't they fed from infancy with the bitter and cherished mythologies of Ireland, the images of self-sacrifice? Christ on his horrible cross, the winsome words of Patrick Pearse and a crowd of other dead heroes. Dan prided himself on his resistance to all those impassioned memories. But his freedom was an illusion. He did not belong to himself. And never had.

He recalled his year in the seminary, preparing for the priesthood. Such an unoriginal aspiration for an Irish adolescent! He had even lived in a cell! That row of clammy dens where the young priests would retire every afternoon to meditate or masturbate. Dan had been snobbish about his own sexual torment, despising the placid virginity of some of the others. The biblical language of possession excited him: 'he took her', 'knew her', 'lay with her'. He was plagued by images of violent, nimble, impersonal sexual acts, but not by guilt. What did it matter if he was weak and bad? Only what is bad can need redemption.

Why did he leave then? Because he grew uneasy about the parallel between his life and his mother's existence? She also immured herself behind high walls. In such a very public privacy.

But that was not all. At that time he believed the claims of Christian theology and they terrified him.

One act of rebellion condemned all mankind.

The murder of one Jew on a cross vindicated all mankind.

Each person is responsible for all others.

It reminded him of the monkey experiment he read about in school. Part of the thalamus was removed from one monkey's brain. When the monkey was placed back in its group, not only was its behaviour altered, but the power structure and behaviour patterns of the others also changed dramatically.

So Daniel was one cell in the body of mankind. Cell, that word again. Sell. Cell yourself. He was a child brought up in symmetrical rooms and gardens, but he would beware the seductions of all systems. He was not a chattering monkey. He began to resist the ecstatic drowning sense that tried to overtake him in church ceremonies. He safeguarded his boundaries.

111

He took to the study of medicine with fervour and vanity. A doctor's life would give him the chance to stand apart and yet fulfil his human responsibility. He would resist evil. He would live a real life. And real life was corpses and bedpans. How brave he fancied himself to be! He saw now that the hospital was his refuge from the intolerable city, an antiseptic heaven full of professorial droning voices: 'Our last lecture stopped at . . . the patient's heart stopped at . . .'

'Oh, I don't want to die . . . "All things long to persist in their being," ' he thought madly, calmly. 'Spinoza. Fuck Spinoza.'

What an idiot he had been to think he could stay out of the 'RA. Like a nun taking up residence in a brothel. Oh, the IRA with their guns and their purchasing power and their rightness and the strength of their utter indifference to death! He would have to wait now. They would come for him. He would tend their injured. He would find out too much. They would dispose of him.

Why must it be so? Why was he so trapped? He thought of his father, who always walked away.

Rosaleen, the superstitious Rosaleen believed that every accident is invited, every negligence deliberate, every chance meeting an appointment. Had he engineered this crisis? McGuire! 'You brought this on yourself!'

'Why am I in this city? The world has so many cities.'

'Man is entirely conditioned by race, environment, and moment in historical time,' he remembered the theory.

'Is this true? This face, this race, this place, is that my doom?'

His fingers played with the non-returnable deposit in his pocket. Why could he not keep his mind properly on the danger? Why did everything seem unreal, out of time? He had a sudden memory of Aidan's funeral. The coffin did not fit in the ground. After some unseemly attempts to force it to lie level, they left it slightly aslant, the top uppermost. Dan kept thinking: 'No, no, it must be the feet raised. Blood to the head, feet raised. Recovery position.'

'And that is how to survive all intolerable events,' he thought. Bestial numbness, denial, and forgetting.

Dan noticed with disapproval a car parked on double yellow lines. He almost smiled at himself. Such a respecter of all minor law . . . How to get through this day? Put the thought of death aside, to think of it later.

A bus was approaching and he ran to board it. He had to stand

112

along with other passengers. A girl's hair began to brush against his hand with every jolt of the bus. He started to anticipate it, liking the rough tickling sensation.

'She knows,' he thought.

She half turned. Beautiful repulsive face.

'If you turn right round, I'll look at you. Smile in a certain way. Say something. It is expected.' He felt suddenly tired and impatient. 'Oh, why is it always like this? This hunger for connection? Anything to get our foot in the door.' As if some stranger wrapping her arms and legs round him could postpone his death! He felt weak in the stomach and knees, as if he might suddenly sob into her pitiless blonde hair.

He remembered the last murder in the district. Of an alleged informer. He was killed slowly and without artistry. Pounded to death with bricks. It was a gradual business, leisurely, a day's work, team-work, with time for tea-breaks and cigarettes.

He remembered Aidan. Oh, Rosaleen! Would she weep more? Or less?

The girl's hair teased against his hand again.

'Flesh and fur,' he thought. 'T. S. Eliot . . . died 1965.'

'What are the dead to do with me?

'What are the living to do with me?'

'Flesh and fur and faeces.'

Don't forget the faeces. *Northern Ireland: The Faecal Society*: subtitle of some book on H-Block. That great reservoir of civilization. Images and phrases recurred to him. Walls daubed with excrement from floor to roof. The high tiring smell of stale urine. Blue-spotted mounds of food decaying in corners. Naked prisoners mired in conviction and shit. Martin Meehan, great daredevil and folk-hero, swathed in a blanket, drawing palm trees with his own excreta. A hobby previously confined to babies and schizos.

'Northern Ireland itself is the Larger Prison,' the eloquent author declared. 'Oh, how will I get out?'

The girl turned towards him. Dan stared at her cold abstracted lovely eyes.

'The smell in the women's prison is even worse than in the men's,' he told her silently, and moved to get off the bus first.

In the street, he paused and looked up at the early evening sky. The only soaring things were the army watch-towers. Suddenly he was

113

terrified of the empty parking spaces. The hospital looked like a place he might never reach. There was a silence, as if the land itself were listening, to hear how he would die.

He broke into a run along the deserted street, keeping his eyes on the bright spots of light from the wards.

He could not be alone any more. He must see Mrs Dwyer.

'Please God, let her be free from pain and visitors.'

Her eyes were closed as he reached her bedside. There was a yellow rose on her table. The drooping petals fell apart at his touch.

'Caught you.' She was awake, smiling up at him.

'I'll get you another. How are you?'

'Drugged. Bored . . . Dying should be more interesting!'

He looked away.

'Oh well. At least you don't tell me I've years in me yet.'

'That would be for my sake,' he said stupidly.

'Of course.'

She began to tell him stories from her past. The private, feverish plans of her youth, her teaching job, her passionate love, her good marriage . . . It sounded like a beautifully plotted novel. Dan wanted to believe it. He *did* believe it . . .

A smile lit her face; a moment of resurrected youth.

'I wasted so much time, though!' she said. 'We're surrounded by cruelty and vulgarity in this place. It crushes out all inspiration! Oh, that's no excuse. I always had a thousand fine excuses! Don't you waste yourself!' she warned him, pointing her admonishing finger, the way she must have done as a teacher. A loving bully of a teacher.

'How will I avoid it?'

'There's no avoidance . . . I'll die soon, won't I?'

'I want to live like you. A good life. A simple, good, intelligent life.'

Dan thought he would break into tears.

'You're a kind young man,' she said, her eyes puzzled and indulgent.

'I don't know what to do. Tell me what to do.'

'I was like you at your age. Always making a great drama out of everything . . . I haven't had the last rites. They seem to be in no hurry. Do you know how much longer?'

He stood up. 'I don't know when any of us will die.' He softened his voice. 'I might be going away soon.'

'Oh?' she spoke coldly.

'Yes. To England, no, America.'

'That's nice.'

'I'll ask them to bring you a cup of tea on my way out.'

'I'm indebted to you.'

He looked back from the doorway. Her lips were moving as if in prayer. He wanted to rush back and say things to her. Beg her to live ten more years, to say one word that might save him . . . But what did she know? She had lived so long and what did she know?

At least, now I'll be able to afford a magnificent wreath, he thought.

## 11

Gerry was soaked with sweat. Every sense was focused in eyes and ears and gun. All feeling was lost in his arms and legs. He itched to press the trigger, to hear the sharp detonation, feel the kick against his shoulder. He kept picturing some grey shadow appearing in the street below, then flopping noiselessly on to the pavement at the firing of the gun. He pictured it so much and so well, he had to blink to see what was really there.

Nothing. Nothing.

It must be late now, beyond his duty-time. Why didn't that cheeky cunt Carter come and take over? *There* was a guy who didn't mind the nothingness. What the hell was he doing?

Lying like a collapsed brick wall in his bunk. Squeezing his pimples. Availing himself of the vast array of recreational facilities. The packs of creased blackened cards. The catalogues of women with big udders and tastefully barbered pubic hair.

Carter always took advantage! The big bastard.

'Just because my arms and wrists are thin. Because I can't get tanked up without spewing . . .' He would arrive yawning, taking insulting slow steps, would not even mention his lateness. 'Not that I'm bitter. Not at all. I only want to kill the bastard.'

Bitter cold. He needed to move. He must move. To stand up, walk down the steps, across the courtyard to his bed, remove his gun, his boots.

And then? Nothing.

He was losing his mind.

Yesterday there was salad for tea, a rare novelty. And on his bed of lettuce, an even rarer novelty. A white worm. For a moment Gerry's eyes went blind with anger at the culinary geniuses who served their food. Then he laughed at the accidental meat ingredient. And then he ate it. That was what he had become. A masticator of worms. God! He wasn't even showing off. No one saw. No one even raised their eyes from the trough when he giggled. He didn't fucken exist, did he? She had forgotten him, that was clear.

Why hadn't she come that night? If he knew, really knew, that she had decided not to come, set her mind against it, then . . . But what if something had prevented her? A thousand things might prevent her. Every day heaviness was filling his whole body, even his head, making it remote from itself. It was a tiredness that could not be helped, that could only go on and on surpassing itself. He loved Rosaleen. His love was the only part of him not dead, not discouraged, not governable. He loved her in spite of every obstacle. Her race, her religion, her hatred, her husband, her absence. He loved the glorious unsuitability of his love.

When he was dropping with weariness, when he was in danger of thinking of her without emotion, he *begged* himself to find her beautiful. Carter appeared before him, silent and sudden as an apparition, but too solid a hunk of meat to maintain that illusion. His face was already grey with cold. No nod, no glance, no greeting. Gerry descended to the yard, his eyelids drooping, sleep stampeding in on him now that he could permit it. He followed the cracks in the clay of the yard, walked through the fatty odours around the kitchen, and entered the hut.

'Rust is everywhere,' he thought. Everything that could rust did.

He lifted the mattress, expecting to see flakes of rust on the wires of the bedframe.

'What you doing?'

It was Des.

'Don't know.'

Des was with Cooper, who was blacking his boots, achieving the mirror-finish with saliva, alternatively drooling and singing. 'The fucker,' Gerry thought, dark splotches dancing before his eyes. Des was lounging on Cooper's bed. Smoking. An ashtray full of stubs lay beside him. There was a mug of cold tea on the locker. Rust-coloured tea.

'Why don't you ever sleep? On your offs,' Gerry asked him with a grudge in his voice. He did not want to start a marathon conversation.

'Can't.'

'Tough.'

Cooper looked up sharply like a keen head-prefect. 'You must

sleep! Report it to the MO. You must keep yourself fit and efficient!
What use is a soldier who . . .'

Des ignored him. He spoke to Gerry. 'This is *my* time.'

'Yeah,' Gerry said without looking at him.

'God, don't let him start preaching!' What was the use of the way
he sat there keeping a frantic tally of every moment of so-called
freetime. He had signed away three years of his life. Nothing could be
clawed back. Gerry prised off his boots. It took a few moments for the
ice of the floor to penetrate his feet. Which stank. It must be really
bad when you noticed your own smell. Really immoderate. He
sneaked a look at Des and Cooper, expecting protests. No. 'So what,
anyway. I stink, therefore I am.'

He pulled back the covers. Methodically. Everything he did was
slow, although he wanted it all to be fast. It wasn't worth removing his
uniform. He got in and pulled the covers over his head. At last. But he
could not sleep.

There was silence in the room. A hard listening silence.

Des did not want him to sleep, that was for sure. But Gerry did not
budge. He would pretend to doze off, and that would make it happen.

Someone stomped into the room, sat down heavily and gave a loud
belch.

'Pig!' said Cooper.

'Wouldn't mind being a pig,' Shiner replied peacefully. 'They have
corkscrew penises.'

'You're a minefield of information!' Cooper said, prim as a tired
tart.

'Shut up,' Gerry yelled.

'Oh, didn't even know you was here! The sleeping bloody beauty!'

Without thinking, Gerry managed to get out of the bed, the
blankets draped around him. He shambled out of the hut, across the
yard, and into the neighbouring hut where he flopped on to Des's
bunk. And slept. The sea came into his dream, the sea, the shore, the
sun. Someone called him and he turned to see only a gold-rimmed
shadow coming out of the dazzle of ocean and sky. A shadow dissolving.

He woke into Des's face. No surprise. As if in his sleep he had
been preparing to find him there.

'I was going to wake you. But you woke anyway.'

Gerry jumped up. 'Is it time?'

'No, not for you. It's time for me . . . I met a girl yesterday. She was pasting up posters of that kid Ruth Kearney that was killed by a plastic bullet.'

'Accident.'

Des laughed. 'I've reached a turning point in my career.'

'It's not fair.'

'No. It isn't.'

'All we get is flak! Makes you sick! We saved them from the Protestants, didn't we?'

Des grinned in a way that irritated Gerry. As if he was the un-abridged *Encyclopaedia Britannica*. The ultra-sensitive bullshit-detector.

'You'll be late,' Gerry warned him.

'I'm already late.'

Des sauntered out, the man of leisure, the aristo. He was the only guy who could manage such a royal walk in DMS boots!

Useless to try and sleep again. Only an hour before he was due back on the roof.

He remembered long ago sunbathing on the roof at home with some girl. Couldn't recall her name.

He turned to rearrange the lumpy pillow and discovered a book underneath it. *British Army Atrocities in Northern Ireland*.

God, if Des was caught with this little volume of bedtime stories!

Gerry thumbed through the catalogue of testimonies and photo-graphs of men with bludgeoned faces and limbs.

There was a section on prisoners who had been given six-month statutory sentences on 'trumped up' charges. 'Yes,' Gerry thought, remembering getting together with two other soldiers to 'organize' the evidence. But they had been told that the men were known terrorists who could not be caught any other way . . .

There was a poem about Bloody Sunday: 'Butchers' Dozen': . . . 'Yet England, even as you lie, You give the facts that you deny . . . priests . . . wagged our blood in the world's face. The truth will out, to your disgrace.' They felt so injured, so *right*. Was he party to a crime? Des had filled the book with underlinings, notes in the margins. Why did he care? He never cared about anything before! He was straight-forward about sex. Never fell in love. Trusted nobody, but was not poisonous about it. Didn't believe in God. Or any mystery. His body was his only pride. His article of faith.

119

'Oh, to hell with it!' he decided, his attention drawn to the sudden pelt of rain against the window. He watched, hoping the water would rinse the panes clean. Maybe the grime was inside?

Nice to be indoors when it was pouring out.

His muscles began to untighten. Some shut-eye maybe? Resisting sleep for a moment, he looked round the hut, recording its details. To try and prevent a shock on reawakening. It was rotten how he never remembered where he was when he first came round . . .

Someone was shaking him, someone was shouting.

'Wake up. Wake. Get up.'

'Leave me alone.'

'Someone's been killed.'

'So what! Let me sleep, will yah?'

'Des, it's Des . . .'

'What? No. No. Who?'

Gerry was on his feet. He charged out into the square.

A stretcher. A covered face. Blood soaking into the clay.

He ran forward and pulled back the sheet. Yanked Des into a sitting posture.

'Stop that.' Hands hauled him away.

'Who? Who?' Gerry kept saying.

'He shot hisself. Accident.'

Gerry ran back to the hut, to Des's bedside. He ransacked the cupboard, taking everything he could lay his hands on, cigarettes, sweets, the money from the wallet, stuffing the inside of his jacket.

'Bastard, bloody thick bastard! You think you can get away . . . You fucker! You stop yourself, that doesn't stop the army. You want to be like Ruth Kearney, innocent and dead, dead and innocent . . . Des . . . Des . . .'

No answer. No answer.

There was shouting and screaming. But it was not him. He did not like the sounds the throat was making. But it did not matter. It was not him . . .

He woke up in an empty room. White sheets, white walls. Temperature chart!

He remembered. Dead. Dead and gone.

Could he have prevented? . . . 'No, I' . . . He hadn't really listened. Even now he had to strain to recall their conversation. If he had been

120

more . . . Maybe it was an accident. It could have been.

No, Des was not some hung-over half-wit who couldn't tell his thumb from his elbow. But he hadn't slept for . . . How long? Weeks . . .

'You'll get all the sleep you want now, you bastard!'

He began to slam his fist against the wall, rhythmically.

Not, non, un, none, gun, gone . . .

It was something to do.

A nurse padded over to the bed. She held out a comb to tidy his hair.

'There you are,' she said.

He watched her face.

'Blue eyes are the worst,' he thought.

Her mouth was bright pink. The mouth said, 'Here, swallow your tablets. They've done wonders for you since you came in here. You want to get better and get out, don't you. Back to your pals.'

'When is the funeral?'

'Hush.'

Two visitors.

The padre. Lumpy gut. Hairline moustache. He was matey, heavily matey. With Gerry and with God Almighty, to whom he brayed loudly.

The doctor. Brisk, busy, but not mean.

'Good news for you,' he said one morning. 'Your mother and father are being flown over.'

'My father is dead.'

'Oh, but I thought there were two . . .'

'My stepfather. My mother married again.'

'Ah, well. Good. Life goes on. Life does go on, you know.'

'The lovebirds are flying to see me,' Gerry thought.

'And you can go back with them. I'm recommending you for a period of home leave.'

'No!'

'But you're not well. Surely you don't want . . . You need to get away from the scene.'

'I'm all right. Honest.'

'You wouldn't be lying there if you were all right!'

Lie down. Shut up. Do as you're told. No. No more. No more.

'Don't send me to England.' There was no plea, no whine in his voice.

The doctor looked as if explanation was dawning on him. 'Is there trouble at home?'

'Yes. It wouldn't work out. Better off here.'

'OK, if you say so. But I'll see to it that you're shifted out of Belfast.'

'No! I've got mates here . . .'

'Ah. Of course!' the doctor glowed, obviously dreaming up pictures of solid gold soldiers offering brotherly support to a bereaved comrade.

'Salt of the earth, my mates, Sir,' Gerry said, making his eyes soulful.

'Good, excellent! OK, you can stay, so long as you're on reduced duties and we can keep a careful watch on your . . . health.'

'Yes, Sir. Thank you very much, Sir.'

The doctor retreated, and Gerry slumped back on the pillow.

'You see, Rosaleen? Now do you see? Faithful unto death . . .'

But there would be no more death. He was through with it, through with the helpless mentality of the soldier. He would get out. And take Rosaleen with him.

## 12

Daniel entered the living room, which looked ghostly and rich, the daytime shabbiness banished by the muted lamplight. Rosaleen turned like a frightened statue, drawing her dressing gown close.

'Oh, I didn't hear you come in!'

He sat down heavily in the nearest chair.

'Don't you want to be near the fire?'

'No, I'm fine.'

Rosaleen resumed her seat and lifted her book but did not open the pages. 'Did you see *The Guardian* today?' she asked.

'No.'

'There was an article about some survey in America. They found that married couples talk to each other for only thirty-two minutes a week, on average.'

'You mean thirty-two minutes a day?'

'No, a week.'

'What else did you do today, besides reading about transatlantic silences?'

Her face was averted from him, cheeks rosy from the heat of the fire.

'Well, I went for an interview . . . for a job,' she said quietly, giving him a look of shy defiance.

He leaned forward angrily. 'What job? You never told me about any job!'

'I thought you would put me off! I mean I thought you would be opposed to it. Oh, I haven't a hope of getting it anyway . . .'

She began to play with the silver crucifix at her throat.

'Why didn't you tell me?' He had meant to adopt the cold tone of interrogation but his voice was gentle and indifferent.

'I'm sorry.'

'I told you not to look for jobs . . .'

'You want me under your thumb . . . Oh, Dan, what am I supposed to do? One day you ask me how many projects for our salvation I have planned, next day you forbid me to seek work.'

'OK. What is the job? Where is it?'

'Playgroup assistant. Unity Flats. Oh, don't look like that! Do you think I want someone to look after my child while I look after other women's kids?'

'If it's just a question of money . . .'

She clicked her tongue in impatience. 'Well of course it is. Don't talk about that, please. It's not as if debts grow less if you constantly talk about them!'

How to tell her: 'We have money'? He could not. He would have to reveal the shameful source of it, the fact that it signalled the beginning of their worries and not the end.

'Unity Flats is so dangerous,' he said at last.

'It was my first interview. First ever,' she said in a child's hurt voice.

He tried to joke with her. 'So it was. Well, how was it? Congenial colleagues, compulsory life-insurance scheme?'

'You think I couldn't cope with it, don't you?'

'No. No. I don't mean to be . . . I'm sure you could.'

'I'm not so sure. It's a grim place. Ugly makeshift rooms. Bleak playground. Someone's plastered posters all over the walls. Cute Disney monkeys embracing. Captions like: 'We're in this together.' Makes it worse somehow. And the people! Very unplayful kids for a start. The organizer quizzed me about my motives for applying. He didn't seem to suspect me of financial desperation!'

'You don't look poor.'

'My mother says you mustn't look poor or you'll get poorer.'

'We'll be all right financially, Rosaleen. You mustn't worry about it.'

'But I do! The organizer kept calling me darling and sweetheart. Does that mean I'm not getting the job?'

'It means he's a bastard! What age is he?'

'Oh, I don't know. About thirty-five. Dangerless pipesucker type. There's a girl working there as well. Red hot philanthropist. She said she tries to create a haven for the local children, a magic circle. I was just starting to like her when she announced that she's an "instrument of God".'

'Well, who isn't in this bloody country?' Dan shouted. 'Every terrorist, butcher, baker, coffinlidmaker!' He covered his eyes with his fists.

'Danny? What's wrong?'

'I'm fed up. I'm tired. I get so tired.'

She sat on the floor and pressed her face against his knees. 'It's the way we live,' she said dreamily. 'The things we're told. Like that God watches us incessantly, knows our most secret thoughts. Every hair on our heads is counted and cherished ... Did you know that children can go bald? So, anyway, it's no wonder we're so self-important! And yet self-negating as well, that's what I don't understand. No one matters, everyone's expendable; they're all so willing to die.'

Daniel held her shoulders and made her look into his face. 'Rosaleen, don't take that job. Stay clear.'

'Dan, you know what I saw today? Some of those kids have been dosed with tranquillizers for years, and they're so dreadfully unsmiling and noiseless. There was one four-year-old girl going bald . . .' She cupped her hand over her mouth, fighting back tears.

'Alopecia?'

'The worst thing is — I don't care. I don't want to do anything. I don't want to feel anything.'

'I know,' he soothed her. 'I know what you mean.'

'But that makes me an accomplice, doesn't it? I'm a part of what produced those sad children? It made me think of when Aidan ... when Aidan was killed. At the time I kept thinking, "Why can't I mourn? Why am I still alive?" And then I started to forget him for longer and longer times. Soon he won't exist at all.'

Dan stopped touching her. 'Is that what we're really talking about? Your dead boyfriend?'

'Oh, for God's sake . . .'

His resentment faded as she started to cry and he held her again.

'Oh, Dan, the day we heard that he was dead . . .'

'I know. I'm sorry. It's just that ... How would you feel if I went around wretched over some dead girl?'

'You do,' she managed to say.

'What does that mean?'

'All the time.'

'What?'

'Over the precious dying patients.'

'You think I don't care for you?'

She hid her face. 'Well, I haven't got the Disease of the Month!'

'I think it's pretty sick of you to be jealous because I care about patients.'

'Care!'

'Someone has to care even if you don't!'

'It's your own death you love in them! You're conquering your fear of it with a thousand previews. And that's not all. You love to be on your feet when other people are on their backs.'

'You're not jealous of them. You're jealous of me.'

'Yes. I'm jealous of your hyper-education. I'm sick . . .'

'You couldn't do what I have to do! You couldn't cope with the sight of suffering and death.'

'I don't flinch from the idea of death.'

'The idea is so much less offensive than the smell.'

'I've seen plenty of corpses. How could I avoid it?'

'Don't try to outbid me. It's not a competition.'

She made a low moaning sound. 'You made me say that. You've made me so cheap and disgusting.'

'Well, you were bound to be contaminated sometime. By my squalor. "Dan's life is so squalid." Quote. Unquote.'

'What are you talking about?'

'I read your diary.'

'I haven't got one.'

'The one you kept before we married. The one replete with Aidan and his breath-taking sayings and your family life with all its holy horrors. I do appear in it from time to time. "Dan's life is so squalid." '

'You have to let me explain. You must listen. I wrote that so soon after I met you. I was afraid of you! I was struggling against your way of seeing things. You saw through everything, through people's motives, you blackened things. You made me feel hopeless.'

'So why did you go on with me?'

'Because you know things, you're not a carbon copy of everyone else. It's the way you look, your air of belonging to a private past. The first time I saw you, it was in church, you were standing before some candles, and suddenly you turned. Your face . . . I felt that feeling like grief and singing mixed up together.'

'Desperation at first sight?'

'Oh don't! I know I haven't loved you enough,' she said, turning away from him.

'Oh God, I wish we could get away from this place,' he groaned. 'It puts such strains on us. Maybe somewhere else . . .'

Rosaleen began to walk to and fro in front of the fire. 'Today in the playgroup I lifted up a little boy, and I felt, suddenly, that I wanted to dash home, lift my own child and run. Get him away before he learns *words*.'

'We will go. Very soon.'

'But how? Why? It's not possible!'

'Rosaleen, listen. I'm borrowing money. That's why I said . . . Well never mind that now. My aunt is lending us some money. Let's use it to get out.'

'But you said you'd never borrow from her!'

'I know what I said. But I was unrealistic and far too proud. There's no such thing as a life without dependence and obligation. It's a question of choosing one's creditors, that's all.'

He tried to quell her excitement, warned her to keep their plans secret, not to buy any new clothes, or even their departure tickets before the day of travel.

Army suspicions were easily aroused by sudden wanderlust.

'You make us sound like criminals.'

'Trust me, don't risk spoiling everything.'

'Could things be any more destroyed between us?' she asked him tearfully.

'We have to get over it. The truth is usually awful. But it clears things.'

'Does it? Maybe it builds as high a wall as any amount of lying?'

He leaned to kiss her, but not on the mouth as if bitterness still lingered there.

'Dan, I never did make love with Aidan.'

'But you wanted to.'

'What would you do . . . if I were unfaithful?'

'You don't know any men.'

'What if it were a man I don't know?'

'I'm a man you don't know.'

'Don't say that. It makes me so lonely. I don't want to go away after all. Let's stay.' She was walking about again, wringing her hands. 'Oh, take no notice. It's madness to stay. And madness to go. Where will we go? Where would we live and earn money? What about your course? We're back to that! Oh, I feel as if every stick of furniture in this room is an obstacle. We'll never get out . . . never . . .'

# 13

'My pussycat likes it when I'm home all day,' Mrs Flaherty announced.

Dan noticed that her legs were planted wide apart, short dress rucked up.

'Don't like cats,' he muttered, knocking back his gin.

'Oh, you'd like mine,' she replied, reaching into her roomy bag, bringing forth a photograph of a sleek, round but undistinguished cat.

'That's my daughter holding him, but it's not a good picture of her, so it's not. I'll show you a real photo of my daughter, so I will. Hang on a sec . . .' She was rummaging through her bag again. 'I've one of her with her husband. He's a good boy, so he is. She could have walked the width and breadth of this earth and not got herself a lovelier husband. He adores me, so he does.'

Daughter and Golden Boy in drab Kodak colour were pressed into Dan's hand. Two brainless grinning faces snapped in the backyard on a rainy day. The clothes on the line behind the lovers flapping in the wind like bunting.

'How lonely you are,' Dan thought with distaste, looking sideways at the woman's fat eager face.

'Very nice. Excuse me, I just . . .'

He went and stood at the bar, waiting for a refill, trying to catch the attention of the barman, who was suave, slow and cold of eye. Dan admired him. 'Barmen have changed,' he thought. 'All of them, the whole breed.' They showed none of the deference, the dazzling prompt servitude they used to bestow on every dole-money splurger who would prop up the bar. Maybe it wasn't only the barmen who were different? He realized that he was wary of nearly everyone. There was a lawlessness about the people, a mockery, a bitter pride. Was it to do with the humiliating presence of troops everywhere?

Wordlessly he pushed his glass towards the barman, who remembered what he was drinking. 'I should go home.' Dan thought guiltily about Rosaleen on her own. He was spending every night until closing time in the pub. For over two weeks he had not been alone, face to face with himself, sincerely. But he could not stop coming here. Even though he disliked his pub cronies, or, at least, they bored him with their dull conversation. It was like a smelly blanket over his head. But he could not leave.

Over in the corner he noticed Marie, her crutches leaning at such an angle on the floor they were like tripwires. 'She wants everyone to notice them; she wants to complain if they notice them; she wants to complain if they forget.'

Marie had fallen down a cliffside and broken her back. People avoided her. They hated her the way the world hates all the irremediably damaged, as if they thought: 'How dare she fall down a cliff?' But partly it was the girl's obsession that kept them away, for she ranted always about the public's attitude towards the disabled, the cruelty, the condescension. She was right, of course, but so what?

He wandered over to her. Her pale face brightened.

'Ah ha!' She turned to her friend. 'Eilis, this is Dan Keenan. Fancies himself as a medic. Do they teach you anything in that hospital besides how to do autopsies? Can you cure anything?'

'I could cure your thirst,' he said, reaching for their empty glasses. 'May I?'

'Smoothie,' she jeered at him, pleased despite herself.

He returned with the drinks, seated himself between the girls.

'I was just saying to Eilis, she's getting to be a desperate size,' Marie said contentedly.

'She looks fine to me,' Dan said, while Eilis bit her lip and would not look at either of them.

'I just couldn't put up with it myself,' Marie declared. 'If I could be a size ten, I wouldn't tolerate to be a size twelve. As I live and breathe, I wouldn't tolerate it. I mean, I have to discipline myself, control my intake. I can't move, can't burn anything off.' She kept her accusing eyes on the unacceptable dimensions of her friend's slender frame.

'Marie,' Dan interrupted. 'I want to ask you a favour. That fireman who was shot accidently at McGill's factory fire . . . you know he has a spinal injury? I was wondering if you would go and see him?'

Marie's lips tightened. 'Let the dead bury the dead?'

'No! Just the opposite! You could help him to see that it's not over. You could help him more than anyone.'

'He's getting plenty of help from what I hear! Twenty thousand pounds in donations . . .'

'Marvellous, I agree! He can't walk, can't go to the toilet, can't fuck, but he can always count his money!'

'Don't you speak to me like that!' she cried out distressfully.

'Sorry.'

She broke the silence first. 'As I live and breathe, I mean, the way I see it, a fireman knows that there's a risk in his work and he accepts that risk. I just don't see why he should get all that fuss and attention, when other people have to manage . . .'

'And just because the world is cruel,' Dan answered her, 'I don't see why that cruelty should be parcelled out equally; I don't see why there shouldn't be some alleviation on some occasions for some people.'

Marie went on gulping down her drink, as if that action were both a reply and a denial.

'For some lucky people,' she said at last, struggling to her feet, while Eilis handed her the crutches.

'You stay here, Eilis.'

'No, I'm coming with you.'

'Stay!' Marie shouted.

Dan and Eilis watched her laboured departure, the crutches tap tapping reproachfully on the floor.

'Exit on stilts,' Dan muttered.

Eilis gave a laugh of relief. 'She is a bit high and mighty!' She looked penitent at once. 'I feel sorry for her, don't you?' she said.

Dan brought them more drinks.

'You're going to be a doctor, are you?' Eilis inquired shyly. 'I think that's wonderful. I always say there are people-people and there are thing-people.'

'Do you now? And what about people who turn people into things?'

Their conversation dwindled to occasional remarks, mostly: 'Want another? Same again . . .' Dan listened to the flute band and the lyrics of the songs. There was one quaint chirpy little number about killing a soldier one bright merry morn. As if bumping off some stray armyman was a frolicsome thing to do in the course of a matinal perambulation!

'We'll get to the dirges later,' Dan thought.

'Hey, do you want to hear a joke?' he said suddenly.

'Oh yes,' the girl replied, eager as a child.

He took a religious tract out of his pocket and read it dramatically:

### 'One Week Too Late

A lady in Scotland became greatly concerned about her soul. One night she was so troubled she could not sleep, but walked the floor in great distress of mind. At last she sat down and wrote in her diary: 'Next week I will attend to the salvation of my soul.' She then retired and slept soundly. The next day she went into scenes of pleasure and gaiety. And the day after she was taken violently ill and soon became delirious. Before her death the delirium left her mind long enough for her to say these solemn words: "I am one week too late! I am lost!" '

Eilis gave him a look of pained incomprehension. 'Where did you get hold of that?'

'From a patient. A Proddie Evangelist. With gallstones. Not syphilis, unfortunately.'

'Oh, in the hospital,' Eilis nodded wisely. 'I suppose you would get all sorts in there.'

Dan lapsed into silence once more. He stared over at Majella, the big barmaid. Her layers of lard were showing through a shiny blouse. Her mouth was a vivid crimson gash. Dan imagined licking off her lipstick, enjoying his sensations of arousal and disgust. Eilis coughed timidly.

'Look at her,' Dan instructed the girl.

'She's grotesque!'

'That's why I like her.'

Eilis looked at Majella again, frowning with concentration like a schoolkid. Dan saw that she wanted to please him, wanted to share what he felt. She took him with such utter seriousness!

He reached over and held her hand with a calculated precision.

She permitted her fingers to lie in his like dead twigs.

'Come closer,' he commanded.

She slouched her Size Twelve against him and he began to kiss her face and neck and hair, drawn more and more to her, liking her odour and her heat.

'I thought you were a married man,' she muttered in his ear, her

131

sounds full of relief and remaining doubt. He did not like her harsh voice right inside his ear!

'Why, that's correct,' he told her with a mean air of congratulation.

'Oh!' she bridled as if her flesh was scorched at all the points of contact. 'I'm going home, so I am.' Her first sure and energetic statement of the entire evening.

'Suit yourself.'

'Playboy!'

'Fuck you,' he thought, watching her clearing off. 'Fuck all of you.' He felt dejected and his eyes smarted. But no tears came. 'My lachrymae are not working,' he decided.

By way of compensation, he became aware of an uncomfortable need to pee. When he stood up, he swayed. His head felt muzzy.

'Too much taken!' someone called to him.

'Not nearly,' he replied, lumbering over to the toilet. 'Not halfways enough.'

He studied the steaming jet of urine. 'Micturition . . . uric acid . . . can be analysed to reveal disease, malfunction . . . Next week I will attend to the salvation of my soul . . .!'

He giggled at his drunken inconsequential thoughts.

'Quick, you're coming with me!' A man he had never set eyes on in his life was tugging at his arm.

'Jesus! Lay off!' Dan snarled, but then grew alarmed at the man's wrathful face. Dan started jabbering, hardly knowing what he said. 'Look, you've got the wrong idea. I'm not of the gay persuasion. Nothing personal . . . You've got the wrong man. I've done nothing . . .'

'You fucken bastard. Move when you're bid. Out the back way . . .'

# 14

'I need more light,' Dan complained.

The face seemed blue. Cyanosis? Or a shadow cast by the half-darkness? A passing car's headlamps gave momentary light to the interior of the van. The faces of Dan's assailants were also haggard and dark.

Dan felt carefully, carefully beneath the injured body for any sign of dampness. Which would signify blood. Which would signify . . . No. None. But the man groaned at every lurch of the boneshaker of a van, every bump in the Godforsaken manforsaken country road.

'Keep his legs raised. Please! Steady.'

He cleansed the hole torn in the stomach as well as possible, plugged it with a crêpe bandage. What more? Nothing.

He leaned close to the man's ear. 'Hold on. Don't sleep. It's all right. Nearly there.'

He hunted the wrist for the pulse. Fast. 160. 180. The heart. Feels solid. But, oh, we know different. Don't think that . . . The heart can stand anything, anything . . .

'Don't shine the light in his eyes!' Dan snapped.

'Sorry!'

There was nothing more he could do now. He began to shiver from the cold, to hear the driving rain on the roof.

He glanced at the two men who had . . . what? Abducted him? The fat dimwit who had accosted him in the toilet. There were tattoos on his arms. The usual harp. A motto which Dan could not make out. Torchlight illumined the babyish down on the man's cheeks. The eyes were meek. But why wasn't he cold? Standing there on his thick sturdy legs. Unmoving. Not shivering at all in this temperature.

'I am trembling and they are not,' Dan thought. 'They are not.'

Dimwit spoke, pointing with his free hand to the whiskey: 'Pass us the bottle, Brendan.'

Dimwit handed him the whiskey with a hospitable gesture. Dan shook his head.

This is it . . . This is it . . . They had come for him. A press gang. They had come for him. As he had expected. No. As he had not expected. He had almost stopped expecting it. Drinking himself paralytic every night. Dulled into . . . dullness. Denial mechanism in full working order. Brendan was glaring at him. The accuser. 'Why aren't you saving him?' Dan had seen that look before around death-beds. As if doctors only let people die out of gross malice!

God, please let him live! What would they do to him if . . . But if he did his best? He could not be blamed? God, the face was so wan and weak! Raising Lazarus would be an easier bloody trick . . .

'What do you think? All right, is he?'

Dan shook his head.

'No?'

'I think there's internal bleeding. Every minute counts.'

'Well, do something?'

'I can't! Godsake! Do you think an Elastoplast and a prayer will cure *that*!'

They eyed each other, exasperated.

'Where are we, anyway?' Dan asked.

'Outside of Lurgan.'

'If you try to make it over the border, he'll die!'

'We'll take our chance.'

'There's the hospital in Lurgan.'

'We'll take our chance.'

The wounded man stirred and began to sigh and mutter. Dan checked the skin of his face. Cold. Moist. The veins in the hands were collapsed. The man's garbled prayers and pleadings filled the van, vying with the uproar of the engine and the crashing rain.

'Stop, please please stop,' Dan thought. Spellbound, the three men watched the labour of the man's death, the long lonely battle of it, until Dimwit began to curse. He cursed the rain, the distance, Dan and his uselessness, he cursed the inadequacy of cursing . . .

Brendan stood watchful and indifferent as God Almighty.

'He is the same age as me,' Dan realized. 'Cast a cold eye on life, On death,' he remembered the poem with a strong sudden sadness. He had missed out, he was excluded from something, a passion, the passion which had brought these men to this blasphemous agony, this race through the dark.

'He's gone!'

Dan checked. Breath, no; heartbeat, no; pulse, missing.

He crashed his fist at the heart. Again. Again.

The lumpy old mattress beneath the body was too yielding.

'Lift him on to the floor! Quick! On to the floor, for Godsake!'

They bundled the man on to the floor, shoving and scraping the mattress out of the way.

'Keep his legs raised!' Dan struck the chest, pausing after each impact to listen. He could hear only his own breathing. His own breathing, his own blood drumming in his ears.

'Oh, it's no use!'

They all stared for a long time. At the body. The corpse.

Then Brendan moved towards the front of the van, rapped at the window to confer with the driver. Dan could not make out their rapid harsh undertones. 'Now what?' he wondered. 'Why are we still rushing on?' But of course they must. With an incriminating carcass on board. But where to now? The disposal plan must surely be different? Disposal! He felt as if everything in his stomach was rising.

Dan went to the tiny squares of window at the back of the van and peered out. The whole countryside lashed with rain and wind, the high half-moon above the dishevelled trees. The van slowed down, making the journey smoother. 'We must have crossed the border,' Dan thought. He gazed now at the familiar country night full of stars and howling wind. It recalled his childhood, when he had lain awake on nights like this, alert for every sound, recognizing them all, especially the mating bark of vixens, so wild with need it made him shiver. Memories. A whole cargo of memories. Who would remember his memories if . . .? 'It must be . . . It must be. You will get out of this.' He would remember his own memories, he would turn this into a memory. 'Control yourself. Control, control.'

Hurled about by the van's movement, he lurched over to Brendan, knelt on the floor. 'I'm sorry,' he whispered. 'There was nothing anyone could do.'

Brendan raised his head.

'Are you ill?' Dan asked him.

'Just knackered.' Quiet voice. No menace.

It was OK. It was going to be all right.

The van turned off the main road and again they were jolted along an uneven track. Came to a halt. Journey's end? Yes. Dan jumped down into the courtyard of a farmhouse. His eyes blinked at the milky dawn sky. Lights came on in the windows of the house. Brendan went to the door and waited until a man dressed in a vest and trousers with hanging braces appeared, vanished again. Returned. A few hasty words. Brendan beckoned.

Inside the kitchen a woman, her face greasy with skincream, was bustling around, rekindling a fire, filling a kettle.

'Come in, lads, come in,' she said, turning to them a face of welcome. 'Youse must be starving. The place will be warmed up before you know it.'

Dan hid his hands in his pockets. The farmer fetched a blanket, handed it solemnly to Brendan, who nodded to Dimwit. They went out.

The farmer turned away modestly and removed his false teeth, replaced them properly. So, that was why he disappeared from the doorway after answering Brendan's knock! Dan felt a rush of sympathy for the man. It was all so absurd. How could anyone be prepared for these dramas?

Brendan and Dimwit returned with the wrapped body. Only the feet in their dirty sneakers protruded. Sickeningly. They were too large and real and personal.

'Over there,' said the farmer, pointing to a corner of the room where there was some space among the brushes and mops.

So, it was OK; he could ask. Dan removed his bloodsmeared hands from his pockets and asked the woman if he could wash.

'Certainly, certainly,' she said, as if ashamed at not divining his wishes. 'Here you are, dear.' She gave him soap and a towel and a winning smile. Like some compliant and pampering hotelier. The brown sticky blood soiled the soap. He cleansed his hands and then washed the soap under the tap. Smells of bacon and fried eggs filled the room. Dan was light and hollow, but he did not want to eat. That presence in the corner of the room, that absence . . .

A mug of tea was thrust to him. Hot and sugared. He swallowed it gratefully. When the food was dished up, Dan refused.

'Here,' Brendan insisted. 'Better get it down you. It'll maybe be a long time to the next meal.'

He sat down obediently and began to taste the food. There was

136

silence while everyone wolfed the breakfast. Afterwards, Dimwit began to roll cigarettes with reverent concentration. He threw one over to Dan.

'No, thanks.'

'You should take up smoking. It helps!'

Brendan stood up, addressed Dan with courtesy.

'Come on out with me. I have to show you the road back north.'

Dan tried to say goodbye to the others, but no one looked up. He followed Brendan outside. They trudged along the gravelled path in silence.

'Are we near Dundalk?' Dan asked eventually.

'Fairly near.'

'Walking distance?'

'Everything is within walking distance if you walk long enough.'

Brendan did not look at him as he spoke. A chill went through Dan.

'What will happen? What will happen now? Please God, don't let . . .'

His senses were jabbed by everything in the surroundings, the dank urinary smell of nettles, the dark dense woods blocking out the sun. A lovely morning without heat or haste. Brendan seemed to notice nothing.

'Where are we going?' Dan thought. 'Going, going, gone.' He remembered the body, the blood that finally leaked out of it like a living thing.

'We'll take a short cut through these trees,' Brendan said.

Dan looked where he was pointing.

'I know this place like the back of my hand.'

'I do not want to go there!' Dan thought, but he went like a dog on a lead.

He remembered suddenly a schoolfriend who had drowned one summer. How their teacher scored a line through his name in the register and wrote 'Deceased' beside it in large letters.

'My wife will be out of her mind with worry,' he said. 'She's all alone with the baby. My son . . .'

No reply.

After a few minutes, Brendan spoke. 'It really bothered you when we lost him. That right?'

'Yes.'

'Why so?'

'It was unnecessary. If we'd gotten him to a hospital . . .'

'When you've got to go, you've got to go!'

'Will you expect me to help you again?'

'Is the remuneration unsatisfactory?'

'I don't want the money!'

'Oh, so you want to help us buckshee? Is this a sudden conversion or what? You never offered your services before!'

'I don't agree with violence.'

'Whose violence? Theirs or ours?'

Dan looked around desperately. 'What if I run for it?' he thought. No, there was nothing to shield him from view. His feet kept stepping one in front of the other. Must talk. He must keep talking.

'I've seen things you don't have to witness. Victims of violence . . .'

'We're all victims of violence.'

'I'm sorry about your friend last night.'

'He was prepared to lay down his life! Ireland will be free one day soon because of the likes of him!'

'Most of the people who die "for Ireland" aren't consulted about it. Where's the freedom in that?'

'You think the Brits will clear out if we ask them sweetly? Somebody has to take them on, while you keep your lilywhite hands out of it. The healing hands . . . You would make a useless doctor! Aye, a wee GP. Nothing but piles and pus.'

'I'll be a surgeon!'

'Never! It takes guts to cut out what's rotten, to decide who's "not to be resuscitated".'

'Like you, you mean?'

'Yes, like me!'

Dan could not see properly, could not hear. For one insane moment, he thought he would knock the man down. He felt himself shouting: 'So what if I'm no good? At least I'm trying to stop people suffering!'

'The wee boy scout with a bandage!'

'I'd rather be that than a wee tin god with a gun! You love it, don't you! What would you be without it?'

'I hate it, you stupid fucker! What do you know about anything? You've never lain for eight hours on a roof waiting. You've never . . . The killing is nothing, you know! It's afterwards. Not going to pieces afterwards.'

Dan looked straight at him. 'Is it really easy to kill someone?'

'Christ! You know the only difference between you and me, fella?'

'No.'

'You haven't come up against any of these cowboys. That's your trouble. I used to be like you, no more harm in me than a fly in the air. Then I was lifted in '76. They broke my ribs, perforated my eardrums . . . Oh, you know, I was treated to all the usual refinements of Brit civilization. I remember being amazed the whole time. That was the chief feeling. How can a man beat the shit out of another man, without anger?'

'There's always anger,' Dan said.

'Still didn't join, mind you. Too scared, I suppose. But then a soldier killed my brother. Shot him dead. Claimed he was a petrol-bomber. They weren't embarrassed by the fact that his clothes and his hands had no trace of explosives! The wee bastard was no more a petrol-bomber than the fucken Man in the Moon! Every time I go after a Brit, I think of James. A soldier killed him, a soldier dies.'

'So you kill people because you loved your brother so much! I see!'

'I execute soldiers.'

'But you never get *the* soldier! That's like making love to a girl with your eyes shut. Pretending it's somebody else.'

'You'd know about that?' Brendan gave him a sardonic look but then laughed ruefully. 'I haven't "made love" for ages. Over two years. All this working unsocial hours . . .'

'The new priesthood,' Dan joked awkwardly.

'I don't want to make love,' Brendan said, his voice suddenly thick with emotion.

'You're Brendan McCartney, aren't you?' Dan said quickly. 'Didn't you escape from the Maze?'

'You're not all that bright, are you, for a scholar?'

'I don't know what you mean.'

'I mean keep your fucken name-guessing games to yourself.'

They fell silent. The ground was spongy. Wet foliage had soaked the bottoms of their jeans. The wood was thinning out now and they could see their way better. They were approaching a lake.

'I used to live in countryside like this,' Dan said.

Brendan seemed not to hear.

'If things were different, I suppose we might have been mates going off for a swim.'

139

Brendan halted so abruptly it surprised Dan, who stopped a few paces ahead.

'This is it.' There was sweat streaming on his face.

'Where are we? We're nowhere . . .'

Brendan took from his pocket a revolver and fired it wildly into the air.

'Christ. Oh sweet Jesus, don't . . .'

'That's what they're waiting to hear back at the house.'

'Oh please . . .'

'Move. Get back north. Thumb no lifts. Get going, you bastard! Move! Move your fucken self!'

## 15

As Captain Reginald Frost steered himself across the barracks square, he pictured his progress like the onslaught of bleach on a dirty sink. Many things offended his observant eyes. Filthy windows, droopy shoulders, tired impolite faces.

No bottle, that was what was wrong with his regiment! This little Irish bunfight was ruining the service. The men thought they were the brave boyos. They felt entitled. Corners were being cut. A whiff of insurrection was in the air. Reginald knew that the road from laxity to mutiny was a straight run. Of course, obviously, it was plainly evident that the Northern Ireland theatre, as it were, was, in overall terms, very small beer indeed. That is, of course, compared to the army's major role as an essential part of the NATO forces in Europe.

At first Reginald had welcomed the Irish fisticuffs as a training ground in combat methods for the men. Reality testing. But it was turning a lot of them into yellowbellies and critical sneaks! And the cut of some of them! As slovenly as the PIRA, that higgledypiggedly bunch of triggerhappy banditos.

Reginald had just come from defusing a bomb lodged in the chimney of a house down in Crossmaglen, which belonged to a young Protestant couple who owned a small farm. The local police had received a very strong tip-off and Frost was called in to look things over. God, what a dump that house was! Clutter and mess. Looked as if a bomb had hit it already. The Irish housewife is a slut. Without exception. Anyway, Reginald found the bomb at last. She was a big beauty, stuck down the chimney waiting to blow sky-high. Not the most accessible of places for the tricky activity of defusing a bomb! He wasn't bloody Santa Claus. But he was an artist. A fine artist. Slow, infinitely patient, timing his dares with exquisite skill. Nobody really appreciated his mammoth courage and expertise. The couple fawned over him, of course, and praised him to the skies in the custom of the Irish when they're not killing you. But they treated him like someone who had removed a domestic nuisance. The man from Rentokil. Still, he knew he was good and that was the main thing. He thrust his hand straight out to demonstrate its fabled steadiness. A passing soldier gave him a puzzled stare. Reginald made the plausible pretence of testing for rain. Rain was always imminent in this piddling country. Oh, it would be so good to get back home!

He was lonely. It was so inconvenient to be a widower. Unhygienic. The demands of the old squirter were giving him more than a soupçon of restlessness lately. Judith couldn't have chosen a worse time to absent herself, as it were.

'No one can help when they die,' he admonished himself. Still, she had always been a saboteur, a subversive influence. She was never punctual, for example. It was a form of disrespect. She favoured passive aggression, whereas he was trained in the military notion of 'awesome violence'. Not only charging full tilt at your target, bayonet ready for the plunge, but bellowing like a mad bull at the same time. Not that there was any opportunity for that sort of thing in Ulster! It was all 'officers and gentlemen', if you please.

'If only the army could get in there and clean up the way they had in Cyprus and Aden! That would perk the men up a bit. And it would drain the colour from the dirty Celtic faces of the populace. As it was, the army's hands were tied. Amnesty, the European Court of Human Shites, the Commie press and media, all squealing brutality every five minutes. And even HMG trotted out its regular reports apologizing for 'excesses'. 'Who is monitoring the PIRA, I'd like to know,' Reginald thought. Excess equals Success. No room for womanish sentiment in these matters. He remembered once seeing a young hawk swooping on an otter. The hawk ate it warm and alive. Total ruthlessness equals total efficiency.

Reginald knew whose side he was on.

Yes, he missed a bit of the theatricals. His martinet approach worked with the squaddies, but it wasn't much fun. He knew how to make them blench and spurt out a load of Yessir, Nosir as copious and charmless as a dose of diarrhoea. But at home they ignored him or laughed in his face.

To tell the honest truth, he had not been happy with Judith. Wrong to speak ill of the dead, but . . . The way she kept producing daughters, not a son in the whole crop. Never a minute's peace after they grew up, all having their monthly dementia at different times.

Staggered periods, ha-ha. Oh, the number of times he had caught Judith saying to them: 'Pass your exams. Then you won't have to get married.' Big incentive!

As if marriage was death itself.

'It's all her fault,' Reginald decided. Take the eldest, Clara. You might as well take her, he thought sorrowfully, everyone else has. She consorted with all kinds of . . . types. She was a teacher of some useless subject. Ancient Chink philosophy or some such mischief. Clara had hated him ever since he threw her white mice in the dustbin. He came home one day and found her blubbering over their retrieved corpses lying on the kitchen table, nasty pink feet sticking up pathetically in the air. (No thought of the germs would cross Clara's high mind, oh, no!) 'But they're vermin,' he kept telling her. 'Vermin!'

She grew into a worshipper of the East and every other fashion. 'But it's Eastern, Dad,' she used to exclaim to him, as if that accidental geographical origin bestowed absolute value on any idea or overpriced bit of ethnic tat. How it hurt him! His daughter, a hundred per cent thoroughbred English, NATO-protected, well-fed, vaccinated, possessing all her teeth plus a university degree, and all she could do was sing the praises of the East. He knew the real East. He had been in the grubby hellholes of the Orient. Dirt and disease, heat and bad smells. Children with flies in their eyes.

Plenty of flies in Clara's eyes too. Unzipped variety . . .

No doubt about it. Judith had been a bad mother and a disloyal wife. Still, she had always tolerated his . . . desires. Nothing doing in that department since he had landed in Ulster. Like trying to draw water from a dry well. Not that he wanted . . .! He wouldn't dip his wick into one of those prolific breeders!

Mind you, it might not be a bad idea to arrange for a mass insemination of Irish women by the British army. Active service, ha-ha. Give them a few hybrids to raise the quality of the race. The Isle of Saints and Scholars indeed! Cromwell got it right: 'The Irish are mere offal, the dregs of mankind.' Members of the United Kingdom, huh! They can't even speak the Queen's English. You have to strain your lugholes to make out their abuse and grovellings. No use trying to beat any sense into them. Civilization cannot be a gift. It takes centuries of evolution. Fact. Historical fact. They're another species. You wouldn't cross the street to meet one of them.

The only famous Irish people are the ones who cleared out early, usually in time to get the benefit of an English education. Like Shaw. And he recommended that Ireland should be sunk to the bottom of the sea. Well, you can't say fairer than that. As for Joyce, he was half-mad and overrated. Dirty old wordspinner, feeling girls' arses in Trieste and churning out his posh porn.

Solution to the Irish problem? Clear the army out. Cut government aid, all transport by sea and air, all communications. Let them boil and toil away in their violence and unreason and superstition. It's their problem after all. Nothing that a little nuclear blast wouldn't fix, ha-ha.

Reginald merited a drink and he felt like company. He liked being with officers and other 'real' men. He liked their rowdy earthiness, although he could not crack any jokes himself and smiles did not register naturally on his face. But that did not mean that he couldn't appreciate a good joke. Internally. Like that one the other day. 'What looks bad, feels good?' . . . 'Vagina.' Now he could almost laugh at that.

Emily . . . He decided to cultivate her acquaintance on his forth-coming leave. Emily was a good clean woman, nice no-nonsense parting in her hair, enough meat on her to get a good grip of. Perhaps a bit mopey since her husband passed on. A sorry incident, that was. Choked on a fishbone in a restaurant. The other diners watched and squealed, spoons suspended, while Henry turned purple and died. Not very circumspect of him to shovel fish into his face without inspecting it first. Extracting fishbones from the gullet seems to be an esoteric skill. You can't rely on people nowadays to know anything handy. Turned out of schools versed in all the red and porno writers, but hardly know how to scratch themselves. Henry was a decent sort, though. Graduate in Frog and Kraut, but OK for all that. Immigra-tion officer trying to stem the flood of 'British' citizens. Finger in the dyke, ha-ha. Anyway, as for Emily — waste not, want not. She had become a little flabby since Henry's demise. A bit hairy and white of leg, into the bargain. You'd think she would bring herself under control. Still, little ol' Reggie would soon iron her out! Presumably she was not a white hot talent in the old heave-ho? But she was young enough to be worth a shot and old enough to be grateful. The project needn't be overly expensive. A couple of meals out, or perhaps one would do it? Italian maybe or Greek? Funny how some gastronomic mishmash laid women on their backs. It was a good move on his part

144

to send her the billet doux just before he defused the petrol tanker bomb. How flattered she must have felt when he was mentioned on the TV news! Yes, good strategy. How to win women and wars. Women should be treated like bombs, he thought. Short delay detonators. There was a particular kind of Irish bomb that reinforced the analogy. It was made of nitrobenzene and weedkiller and gave off an overpowering and wonderful smell of almonds. Just like a woman with her beguiling scents.

Reginald could perform the same trick at work and play. You had to walk up to them (bombs and females), fix them for good and all, and walk away unscathed.

It was precisely 13.00 hours. Time enough to give the once-over to the goings-on in the office before scooting off for a drink. He sat down at his desk, already mentally composing his report on the defusal. It would be crisp, understated, no flourishes.

There was a knock at the door.

'Enter.'

A squaddie appeared and swaggered up to the desk. Swaggered. No other word for it. Nothing worse than a prole with a sense of grandeur.

'Number?' Reginald said icily.

'790865, Sir.'

Reginald surveyed the specimen. Cap not at right angles. Pulled straight back from the brow in the fashion of Basque terrorists! Big Hong Kong gadgety watch. Was there a hint of red T-shirt beneath the combat jacket? Too chummy-chummy. A reasonable man expecting to meet other reasonable men!

And there was something else about that foolish face. The boy looked half-animal, half-saint, as if the two sides of him were hammering it out in a boxing ring. Reginald knew the type. He knew all the types. There were only five types of human, after all.

This was the type who spawned a dozen bad poems under the whip of common lust. The type who wouldn't be seen dead in a football crowd, but would lap up every minute of a match on TV. Full of personal pride. No pride at all in his uniform, regiment, country, monarch. Reginald felt the ire blaze in his patriotic soul.

'Would you sign my duty report, Sir? Please, Sir?'

Reginald perused the hand-written sheet. Not one of the i's was dotted. The soldier was obviously the excretion of a comprehensive

145

school. He handed it back and intimated that he would consider reading it when the i's were not so denuded.

Two minutes later the private returned and handed him the paper again. Trustingly. Reginald looked.

Each i was now topped with a flamboyant circle, big as a halo and twice as insolent. Not even good circles. Wonky ellipses that might have been executed by a drunken ape. Reginald did not bat one eyelid, budge one muscle.

'I want this thing typed.'

'I'm off duty, Sir.'

'I don't think you heard me, soldier.'

'Rightaway, Sir.'

Reginald regretted his demand at once. Now he would have to hang around waiting for the young hooligan to tap out his illiterate report with two fat futile fingers. It would be too late then to go and relax over a drink. So, he was to be deprived even of his moderate alcoholic refreshment. No justice in this world. Refreshment . . . The word made him think of long drinks afloat with tinkling ice, waves crashing on beaches, cisterns emptying themselves thunderously. Toilet. I need the toilet, he realized. He stamped over to the nearby pisshouse, where he donated a half litre, aiming even the last droplets successfully into the bowl. He was a neat pisser, unlike some. The foul cumulated odour of the place depressed him but he lingered there, still in the voiding posture.

That boy had upset him. There was something in his . . . attitude. A sort of lazy respect, yes, the kind of oh so bored respect which the sight of decrepitude compels. God! The nerve of it, looking at me like that. What does he know about anything, that fool of a boy, that dunce. Probably had his forefinger dipped more often than his foreskin!

Reginald felt a fit of weepies coming on . . . Well, almost. 'I'm overtired,' he told himself. 'Everything is left to me. No other officer bothers about discipline. It's all "Spare the rod".'

He looked down at his own neglected faintly tumescent rod. Fingered it wistfully. God, what an awful country! What a bloody life!

'Here it is, Sir,' said the squaddie. Wary this time.

Reginald ripped up the report without a glance. Waited.

146

No whimper of dismay.

Minutes dragged by.

Reginald was biting his inside lip with impatience, but the squaddie's face remained frozen and superior, as if the little swine was sure of moral victory no matter what! 'Your uniform is a disgrace.'

No reply.

'Well?'

'I was lying on the roof. Sir. Not very clean up there. Sir.'

'I said your uniform is a disgrace. What is it?'

'A disgrace. Sir.'

'*You* are a disgrace.'

'Yes. Sir.'

'What are you?'

'A disgrace. Sir.'

'Louder!'

'A disgrace. Sir!'

'So glad we agree. Report to me at 16.00 hours for full kit inspection.'

At last, pallor was induced.

'I trust that does not interfere with your social calendar.'

'No, Sir. Thank you, Sir.'

'Dis. . .missed,' Reginald sang out, with a strange reluctance, as if savouring the last mouthful of a good meal.

The soldier saluted and walked out, humble and resigned.

Ah well, there was the next interview to look forward to. And prepare for. Reginald unlocked the cabinet and found the file: Gerard Harris. Always a good idea to gen up on the squaddies. The trick of sudden allusion to some intimate detail of a soldier's background could really stun the pathetic sods.

Reginald the Omniscient.

He flicked through the pages. He did not like what he read there. No indeed, he did not relish this one bit! Harris was hospitalized after the death in a shooting accident of Private Sinclair. Threw a screaming hysterical fit. The two men were friends from the same town. Joined together. Harris had broken down completely for a time. Big crybaby. Now functioning OK, but had applied to buy himself out.

Reginald was very uneasy. Such excessive devotion, such an unmanly show of grief . . . Unmanly! Yes, that was it! Joined together, ha-ha! A couple. A copulatory couple! Nasty little pederasts. At least Sinclair had done the decent thing, eliminating himself. 'I thought as much, yes, I thought as much,' Reginald crowed to himself. That silky sneaky look. Little cheat joining the army for a life of "action"! Hoping to acquire a harem of hairy arses to stick it in! Subsidized by clean-living taxpayers. The Captain had a sudden vision of Harris buggering away deeply and cheerfully . . .

Reginald had an erection.

He tried to disown it.

He tried to will flaccidity.

But of course it had nothing to do with these . . . ah . . . thoughts. Nothing whatsoever. There was no connection.

Yes, yes, that was the trouble, of course! He had had no 'connection', ha-ha, for some considerable time . . .

# 16

Noisy breathing, a trail of dribble out of the corner of her mouth. Silence.

'Moving. It was very moving, wasn't it?' mumbled Dwyer, wiping his forehead.

Husband and son stood at opposite sides of her bed, large and awkward like farmers in mothballed city suits.

'She didn't linger,' said the son.

'She's been in hospital this two months and more,' Dwyer reminded him.

'With respect, I was referring to the final end, I mean, she didn't linger at the final end . . .'

'I'm glad you managed to get here at the last. Though she didn't know it, God help her. Always had the soft spot for you, aye, the eldest . . .' he trailed off, meek but with a hint of accusation.

'The job keeps me on the go, you know, a lot to attend to. Anyway, I durst not leave the house and Patricia on her own. They don't call it bandit country down there for nothing, so.'

The father waved his hand to quieten him. They stared at the dead woman as if they did not know what to do or say next.

The son spoke first, shamefaced: 'Da, what about the . . . have you made the arrangements?'

'No, no, I haven't been able to think . . .'

'With respect, you must have seen it coming!'

'Ah well, there's her family plot out at Limavady. There's room . . .' his voice caught.

'That's useless. How can you have the whole connection traipsing out to Limavady, have a heart. Have you thought of cremation?'

'Oh no! I don't hold with these modern ideas . . .'

'It's far cleaner, Da! And it's great for cutting down on expenses.

No ground to buy, no monument, no burial fees, cuts out all the palaver!'

'But! . . . There'd be nothing left of her!'

'People can't go in for burial the way they used to, Da. Think of the cost of living! Hey, the cost of living, that's a good one, eh?' he appealed to Dan with a quick sour laugh, then resumed wearily: 'Anyway, you're never burying her away out in Limavady. Didn't she spend her whole married life in Belfast?'

The old man rubbed his eyes. 'Aye. Thirty year and more.'

Again silence. The son stood there, truculent, eyeing his father, willing a decision.

Dan wanted them out. A debate on the pros and cons of cremation could be carried on elsewhere, he thought.

'Would you like to come along to Sister's office?' he suggested. The son's eyes brightened at the prospect of tea and feminine sympathy.

Dan walked along between the two men, leading the bewildered Dwyer senior by the arm, while the son glared like some brattish kid, as if he wished he had thought of that first.

Flanked by their two hulking forms, Dan felt sharp and lean. Funny how big graceless men could never cope with anything, he thought. Father and son had the same wet weak mouths, the same flabby unimpressionability in their faces.

He installed them in the office, returned to the bedside, the contained anger starting to rise in him. 'The cost of living!' he repeated to himself. And that fake appeal to sentiment: 'Didn't she spend her whole married life . . .?'

Her married *life*! Contradiction in terms . . .

That countrified oaf of a son would get his own cheapskate way, Dan knew it.

He relented when he looked at her. He had avoided looking, properly looking before, waiting until they were gone. He had to be unimpeded by their rights, their rigidities. Her skin was taut, making the bones gleam through.

Her face calmed him. She had the same influence still.

He realized that it did not matter what happened to her now, whether she was burnt or dumped in the stupid soil beneath a hunk of stone. The incident was closed, as they say. Closed. He touched the stack of books on her bedside table: the *Oxford Book of Verse*, the

150

collected works of Blake, Eliot's *Middlemarch*. Her final ambition had been to re-read the novel right through before . . . But it was too heavy for her to hold.

She read only English literature, he noticed. 'The British are not all barbarians,' she had said to him one day.

'No, no, I daresay,' he conceded. 'And even the thugs that are here, the English gents that kill children with plastic bullets, wreck houses, gun down unarmed people, I'm sure they're all devoted sons and fathers and virtuous citizens.' Dan grew more incensed; it was like a kind of rapture. 'There have been more than a hundred killings of ordinary people by the so-called security forces since the army came here. Only twelve soldiers have been prosecuted and nine of them were acquitted!' He went on speaking, feeding himself on that bitter nurture, that set menu, each atrocity recalling another, as if the dead were queuing up to be remembered, named, assuaged.

Mrs Dwyer had watched his face closely. He became aware of her scrutiny and of his own voice, a voice he had heard in others, raw, plaintive, curiously proud.

'Excuse the oratory,' he tried to dismiss it.

'Are you always ashamed when you get carried away?'

'Yes.'

She waited.

'It's not honest. You have to leave things out, or call our terrorism by another name, before you can . . . I don't want to be a specialist in moral indignation like everyone else!'

' "Our" terrorism,' she repeated. 'Do you associate yourself? Are you in it in some way?'

He hesitated for a moment, thinking of Brendan. He would have loved the relief of telling her about him, how Brendan had confused the issues for him. That he could not disrespect or dismiss him.

He said: 'In my spare time?' As if it was a joke.

'No. No. I just wondered if you often talked that way about army brutalities. It would be inflaming to others. Your contribution, as it were.'

There was no trace of condemnation in her voice, but Dan's face flushed. 'No, of course I don't,' he said, trying to remember if he had or not. 'I hate that kind of talk really . . . I don't . . . There's such glamour in it, all this perpetual pain we live in. We're an elect race like the Jews, with the same genius for suffering. It's a lie. Misery isn't beautiful and ennobling.'

'More oratory?'

'I don't know.'

'You seem full of sadness, that's for sure. It's rare to see you smile.'

'Seduced by sorrow,' he said.

'Infected,' she corrected him.

It was time for him to leave. The nurses arrived to lay her out for the final peepshow. They whispered and padded about, anxious to remove the waxen embarrassment before it could ruin the tranquillity of breakfast for the other patients. One of the nurses called him before he reached the door: 'Hey, you're Daniel, aren't you?'

'Yes.'

She was holding a transparent plastic bag into which she had already flung most of Mrs Dwyer's possessions. 'Look,' she said, indicating one of the books on the table, 'there's an inscription to you on the flyleaf. She must have intended you to have it.' She gave him an inquisitive look.

He took the book without a word and walked off. For no reason his heart started to bang.

Alone in the toilets, he examined the volume. It was the Blake. His eye raced over the writing. Just three lines. 'Daniel Keenan, thanks for everything.' And underneath: 'See pages 23, 47, 126, 198.' He checked those pages. She had marked lines for him. Passages in the *Songs of Innocence and Experience*. He did not read them; he would mete them out to himself.

Back to the inscription. 'Daniel Keenan, thanks . . .' No, it read: 'Thank'. She had left off the 's'. The mistake touched him absurdly. The handwriting was faltering, like a child's.

How she must have struggled to do it! With her faculties failing, her tirednesses becoming longer and deeper. He went over to the window. The bright silver winter's day seemed lovely now, not merciless. She was near him. Their conversation would last a little longer. She had wanted to leave him messages. Why Blake?

He remembered the account of Blake's death, how his eyes had suddenly brightened and he had sung of the things he could see in Heaven . . . Oh nonsense, Dan checked himself. 'The brain was fevered.' But the image came back, a man with magnificent enraptured eyes singing on his deathbed. Singing!

Suddenly Dan knew something. She had made no mistake. She had left him an instruction. 'Thank for everything.'

God, his own brain must be fevered!

But his spirits lifted.

She's dead, she's dead, he told himself, wanting to douse the lightness of heart.

The tree outside, although it was so still, seemed to stretch up, pointing its dead bare branches. It quivered in the bright air.

'Everything is all right,' Dan thought.

## 17

They took a taxi to their host's mansion on the Malone Road, the untouched area of Belfast, resplendent with spacious houses, big cars resting on their laurels in driveways, closely shaved lawns, sanitary high-class dogs, children with good teeth, fat joggers doing penance for business lunches. It was peaceful and Rosaleen found herself breathing more comfortably. As they alighted from the taxi, she had a sudden feeling of awe and spite. How could these people live so well in the midst of murders and the daily torturing of suspects? But what did she, Rosaleen, do about torture? Rush out and fling herself into the arms of one of the perpetrators, that's all ... Their hostess opened the door to greet them.

'Oh hello, do come in! You came in a taxi. Brave things! I had such a frightful experience coming home from the airport last week in a taxi. Of course I *know* one shouldn't use taxis after dark, but how on earth is one to get home! Anyway, this beastly little driver simply would not stop at the house! I banged and banged at the window, watching his dreadful head crouching over the wheel, so sinister! I was convinced he was one of those ghastly sectarian assassins. I can't tell you how much he looked the part!' Throughout all this chatter, she removed their coats, summoned a waiter over to Rosaleen and whisked Dan away.

Rosaleen clutched her sherry and hoped that no one would talk to her. The women were eyeing each other like so many aesthetic phenomena, awarding points. They were all wearing daring dresses topped by grave faces, which seemed to emphasize that the bare flesh was strictly for visual appreciation. Rosaleen, without display of cleavage, cosmetics, or good-taste jewellery, would have felt like Jane Eyre at the ball if it were not for her untrammelled mass of hair. 'God, I wonder if men know that women dress for other women?'

She straightened her spine, advanced her chin. Suddenly she noticed Eleanor McBride, who was clad in an outfit that made her look like a pasha's concubine. Baggy chiffon trousers, bare waist, breasts swathed in two silk scarves, a veil framing her face. A hard-working scene-stealer, isolated for her pains, Eleanor stood in the centre of the room giving little vampish looks which elicited no response. She began to look very unhappy.

Steve McBride, Eleanor's husband, came over to speak with Rosaleen. He was Dan's colleague and a formidable academic rival.

'Have you complimented my wife on her costume? Have you told her how lovely she looks?'

'No.'

'No?' he repeated, feigning amazement.

'Am I failing in my social obligations?'

'Most grievously.'

'Eleanor *is* lovely. She'd look lovely in a boiler suit.'

'What is that supposed to mean?'

'Nothing. She'd look lovely in anything, that's all.'

'You don't like her costume.'

'Yes I do. I just think it's a bit absurd. I mean out of place.'

Steve scowled, then laughed loudly. 'As a matter of fact she's a rather absurd girl. How shall I upstage her? I was thinking of flirting with men tonight instead of women.'

'I'm sure you'd be very successful.'

'Don't know how to take that!'

'Who will you approach first?' Rosaleen asked him. 'Who do you find irresistible?'

'Ah, that's the problem! I don't find anyone irresistible.' He leaned close to her face. 'Not even you and your "refreshing" forthrightness and your blue-eyed countenance and your modest wee frock right down to below your knees.'

Rosaleen bit her lip. 'I'm sorry I criticized Eleanor. I had no intention of offending you.'

'Don't ruin the effect! I prefer to see you untroubled by the desire to please. Eleanor tries too hard in that department. Like your dear spouse.'

'I don't know what you mean.'

'Oh no?'

'No!'

'Take a look at him. Jawing with Marcus Hogan. No one talks that much to Hogan unless there's advantage in it.'

'Dan likes him. He respects him!'

'Take a look round the room. All the career-climbers are on Dan's side of the room. The sex maniacs and serious boozers are on our side.'

'Well, I'd rather you included Dan in the first category!'

'Point is, your Danny Boy doesn't have to bother so much. You've only got to be a Catholic nowadays and it's all handed to you!'

'What rubbish! For Godsake!' Furious conceited phrases surged through her mind, but she did not know what to say.

Eleanor appeared before then, unaware of their friction. 'Hello, Stevie!'

'What is it about him?' she appealed to Rosaleen. 'Do you think he's handsome?'

It was as if she suspected she had lowered herself by marrying him, and needed someone to explain his attractions. She grabbed her husband's hand and pressed it against her naked belly.

'See,' she said mournfully to Rosaleen. 'His child is moving and he is unmoved.'

'Are you pregnant?' Rosaleen was startled out of indignation.

'Yes, God help me!'

'It's masculine, not divine help you need, Eleanor, in order to achieve pregnancy!' Steve interrupted.

'I don't like you!' she snapped, flouncing off.

While Steve stood spellbound watching Eleanor's departure, Rosaleen slipped away and went over to the window, from where she watched the forays on to the loaded buffet table. Dr Kerr was feasting himself on watermelon shaped like a gigantic grin. The luscious wholesome fruit disappeared at astonishing speed into his sallow face. His concentration pleased her. Everyone else pretended that the food was secondary to the exchange of platitudes, risking discreet little nibbles while they maintained eye-contact with the person inflicting conversation.

Suddenly Steve was standing beside her again. He offered her a dish of pistachio ice cream, as if it were an oblation.

'This has to be for you!' He gave her a sweet smile.

She accepted the dish, completely charmed.

'Reminds me of you. Green and cold. And unusual. Until you taste it!'

'Oh! Why are you ..? Please leave me alone.'

'Can't. I'm bored.'

'Boring!'

He wagged his finger at her. 'Temper!'

She was relieved to see Dan making his way over to them.

'Come and meet Marcus Hogan, Rosaleen.'

'Have you taught her how to curtsey?' Steve said.

Dan ignored him.

Professor Hogan greeted her with an air of hospitality. She pressed his thin cold hand. 'So you're married to this brilliant young man . . . charming.'

'He has a high opinion of you also.'

He waved his hand, self-deprecating but pleased. 'I have some good news for you, my dear. We've decided to award your husband the Hugh Daly prize for his dissertation on wasting diseases!'

'Oh, that's great. Congratulations, Dan. Isn't it terrific?'

'I'm just leaving you two for a moment,' said the professor. 'I'm going to organize some champagne.'

Rosaleen and Dan stood together like shy strangers. She wanted to say 'You didn't tell me you were writing a dissertation', but she checked the impulse. Perhaps he had told her and she had forgotten. Then he would be annoyed. But no, she was sure. 'You have secrets,' she thought. 'Did you expect this?' she asked.

His reply was cool. 'Well, people said I would get it. I never thought much about it.' Did he really feel no pleasure, no triumph?

'You deserve it. You deserve it so much!' She thought she might cry.

He flashed her a look that was almost distraught.

Suddenly she desired him so ardently. The air between them felt tight with her longing. The noise and commotion around them seemed to retreat. She could not wait to go home with him. They would be alone. The dark room, the warm bed . . . She would speak his name in a certain way. He would be arrested by something different in her voice . . . She turned away in shame. There must be a look of perfect lust on her face! Why could she not be like these other women? So pure and blonde and bloodless. There was nothing messy about *them*! Dan was brilliant. His very brilliance placed him beyond her. Having a child had made her weak. She had lost her courage. While *he*, he had become stronger. Yes, adversity had made him

157

stronger. She turned to face him again. 'God, I love you,' she thought.

'It's a pity they never play that piano,' she said brightly. 'I'd play it every day if I lived here!'

'Listen,' Dan whispered to her, 'Hogan's going to do an announcement and a toast. Stay beside me and do your "jaded celebrity" look!'

His touch and his conspiratorial voice cheered her.

'Shall I?' she practised a slightly arched eyebrow and a downturned mouth.

'Too much,' he laughed.

'How about this? "Subdued delight"?'

'Yes, that's it!'

He pulled her briefly against him. 'The unsubdued delight comes later,' he promised.

How long did they stand there? She did not know, but when people flocked around them to congratulate Dan, it did not seem an intrusion. She looked happily at the circle of beaming faces. 'Friends,' she thought. 'These are our friends.'

A new life was beginning.

As people drifted away again, Steve sidled over.

'Lost his pale stricken look now, hasn't he?' he spoke to Rosaleen, but kept glancing at Dan to test the effect of his goading. 'Did he tell you his favourite patient snuffed it yesterday? Very close, they were. Attached, you might say. His trouble is, he treats the ward like a little friendship club.'

'And you treat it like a meat factory!' Dan said.

'Oh, I say, that's a bit harsh. Just because *I* don't have philosophical discussions with geriatrics at the gates of death. And what did you learn from your little Catholic granny?'

Dan's face darkened and his speech became jerky: Rosaleen knew it was a sign of rage in him. 'She talked more sense than any of the gurus you chase after! Christ, you fall at the feet of every twinkle-eyed self-appointed deity that ever had a Swiss bank account.' He adopted a lisping Indian accent: ' "Avoid all conflict. Avoid all thought." It's no wonder your brain has turned to mush!'

'Well, and what if it has? There are no rewards for intelligence in this faculty. Brains are no weapon against favouritism!'

'Oh, I see,' Dan shrugged. 'The bloody prize!'

'Don't overdo the coolness act! Oh, six hundred pounds for a trip to Europe! And a step up in your career. Mere trifles, yawn, yawn.'

'You attach a great deal more significance to it than I do.'

'And why would that be? Does it offend your principles? I suppose winning prizes is fatal to the equality of mankind?' Steve jeered.

'Oh no, I don't believe in equality when I look at you.'

'Fenian bastard!'

'Get your man a drink, Eleanor. Bitter orange.'

'I'm going to get you, Keenan. You're finished.' He made a move towards Dan, fists clenched.

'Stop it, you're drunk,' Rosaleen pleaded at him.

Eleanor tried to usher him away.

'Wait a minute,' Dan said. 'I have something to say to you! I didn't get that prize off Santa! I achieved something by effort that you think should be yours by birthright. Well, wake up, kiddo, those days are over! And in case you haven't noticed, I'm more welcome in this suffocating Protestant drawing room than you and your Mrs Zelda Fitzgerald there!'

Marcus Hogan, who had been listening unnoticed, stepped forward, white-faced with distress. 'Stop this at once! If you two young men want to conduct a brawl, go to some public house where they may be accustomed to such scenes! I am profoundly disappointed. To hear you, Steven, account for your failure by alleging discrimination! To hear the words "Protestant" and "Catholic" spat out like curses! By two people who aspire to be doctors!'

He turned to Daniel the face of a hurt friend: 'I'm sorry you find my home "suffocating". There will be no necessity for you to enter it again.'

They walked along hangdog like children expelled from school. It was Dan who spoke first. 'I wish I was dead. Don't suppose it's permanent.'

'What? Death?' she said wildly.

'My present desire for death.'

She burst into tears and he led her over to sit on a bench in the university quadrangle.

'I'm sorry, Rosaleen. God, it all started out so well! What will I do about Marcus? It can't be mended, can it?'

'Those days are not over,' she murmured, not listening to him.

159

'What days?'

'Oh, nothing's changed. Nothing will ever change in this place. You can be clever and dedicated and never shake your fist at them, it makes no difference! We were humiliated because we're Catholics! Fenian upstarts ... Turfed out of that bloody palatial fridge of a house because you wouldn't let McBride abuse you!'

'Don't be bitter.'

'I am bitter! Oh, I know your professor thinks it's a vulgar low-class aberration. What does he know about our lives? I do hate Protestants. God, I hate them! You know what I kept remembering tonight? Not just when you were quarrelling, but when McBride was following me around, leering.' She looked at Dan anxiously.

'Go on.'

'Every twelfth of July Orangemen used to walk over Tait's Bridge, you know? Stomping like a crowd of mad Zulus with their bloody Lambeg drums booming like thunderclaps. They threw pennies down at us. And shouted things. Obscenities ... And one year there was this ugly lout who looked at me. At me in particular. In *that* way ... you know, as if to say, "I can have you any time." '

Dan stood up and walked a few paces.

'Dan?'

'I'm listening to you!'

'The worst thing was the way I felt. Sort of scared and servile. And something else. Nearly like worship ... No, not worship! They were so certain ... They owned everything ... The power was all theirs and they knew it. Oh, I can't explain.'

He sat down again, pressed his fingers to his eyelids.

She broke the silence at last: 'Dan, will they still give you the prize?'

He gave a queer strident laugh. 'Yes, it wasn't an award for social grace!'

'What did you get it for exactly?'

'Ha! A series of case histories on multiple sclerosis. Which means that I monitored a few deaths in the making, gradual and horrible deaths. But my dissertation is a joy to read! Precise, eloquent, useless. Listen, I'm in a ratrace! Medics carve up patients all day, then they start on each other. What you saw tonight, that bigotry, is just a handy extra, it's not what it's about ... God, I wish I was out of it!'

'Oh no, Dan, not again!'

'I don't belong there.'

'Croppies lie down!'

'I told you that's not what it's about!'

'You're afraid to face Marcus, that's all.'

'When my mother died, I didn't feel anything, except "everything is down to you now". There was only me and everything was down to me! I'm sick of my own ambition!'

'You're not on your own now! If you ask me . . .'

'I'm not asking you!'

Silence again. She was dreadfully tired. It was too much to take in, too confusing, the way they had slipped from that moment of proud success to this . . .

Why was he dredging up the old doubts about becoming a doctor? Why did he dismiss his work? He did not profit from illness, that was nonsense!

If he was sick of his own ambition, well, she knew what he meant, she understood the difficulty of carrying your own individual purpose. Sometimes it was like trying to fly a limp kite. But he could not drop ambition and sprawl around! Didn't he always say he would not run with the pack? That was what she loved . . . But maybe he was running with a pack, an élite pack? Was that what he meant? A stab of resentment went through her. He had ruined everything tonight! Consciously or unconsciously? He had no right to be unconscious! He should have ignored McBride, not risen to his bait. 'I blame you, I blame you!' she thought inwardly.

Dan sighed and rose, startling her.

'Come on, we've got to get home.'

'How?'

'Walk.'

'Oh no, it's far too dangerous.'

'Oh, come on, nothing more can befall us tonight.'

'Please get a taxi.'

'I'm too restless. I need to walk.'

Two miles across the dark deserted city. No sound save for the ringing of their footsteps, the drone of an occasional car. Rosaleen felt every nerve in her body taut with fright. Each car seemed to slow down as it approached them. Every doorway, every alley was concealing . . . something.

At last they reached their street and, of course, soldiers halted them. The usual battery of questions in bored English voices.

'Where are you going?'

'Where have you been? I see, midnight revellers! What is the name of the person who gave the party? And the address? Why were they on foot? Which route had they taken across town? Weren't they pushing their luck?'

Dan gave calm careless replies. They had made him spreadeagle against the wall for frisking. Rosaleen watched while they searched him, her eyes scalding in protest. Dan's body was bent forward, rump jutting out like a female baboon inviting sexual entry.

'You didn't need to go through this!' she told him silently. 'Why didn't you call a taxi!'

Dan did as they told him. And the soldiers, in their turn, did what they were told. Oh, if only some gesture of hers could free them all from this hideous obedience!

It was over. The soldiers seemed relaxed and friendly now, as if they were grateful for some distraction in the blank stretch of their night.

'Let me give *you* some medical advice, Mr Keenan. Night-time strolls can be terminal. Goodnight, Ma'am. Sir.'

They collected the baby and Rosaleen carried him as carefully and respectfully as a box of gelignite, determined he would not waken.

Dan sat drinking tea, lost in thought. His face was beautiful. It made her sorry for all her rancorous thoughts.

'I'm not a very nice person.'

'You'll do,' he said.

She did not trust this. They were always approaching each other, veering away again.

'I want to get more out of life,' he said suddenly.

'Yes. Do you? Oh, so do I.'

She sat on the floor, resting her head against his knees. He told her about Mrs Dwyer, about their friendship, her death, the things she had said to him. Rosaleen felt herself drifting helplessly on the stream of his soft voice towards an unbearable sadness.

'I can't lose her and Marcus as well,' he said finally.

'It'll be all right with Marcus.'

'Mummy and Daddy,' she thought, ashamed at once. He must not see her jealousy! But oh these strangers who made up the meaning of his life! She stood and went to the window. There was a dog's hollow barking in the distance, a melancholy sound.

Dan was fiddling with the radio, trying to find a station.

'Don't waken Louis.'

'No, I won't. I'm trying to catch the news.'

Strains of Country and Western music filled the room.

'That's it!' she said. 'Radio Ulster. C. and W. twenty-four hours a day. Simple music for simple folk!'

'Just a couple of minutes,' he smiled.

'This is Radio Ulster. Here is the news at two o'clock, the twenty-sixth May. Brendan McCartney, who was arrested yesterday at Crossmaglen under Section 10 of the Emergency Provisions Act, was found dead earlier tonight in a cell at Gough Barracks. McCartney is alleged to have taken his own life by hanging himself from a ventilator shaft. A medical examination of the prisoner was performed both before and after questioning. Foul play is not suspected.'

'Oh no! Dan shouted, his face crumpling as if he were in pain.

Rosaleen rushed to switch off the radio. She stood over Dan, who was crying, ugly rasping sounds, words, non-words.

'What? My love, what is it? . . .'

'The bastards . . .' he choked.

'Do you know? How can you know him? You can't possibly know him . . .'

'They've killed Brendan! Oh my God, they've killed Brendan.'

'What is he to you?'

Dan regained some calmness. His face was hidden by his hands, his shoulders showed no movement of breathing.

'Who is he, Dan? Answer me.'

Bitter desire like hatred made her flesh shiver. She prised his hands from his face. 'Love me! You have to love me!'

He looked at her as if he had forgotten her. She dropped his hands and fled into the kitchen, banging doors in her clumsiness.

'What will happen now? What has happened?'

The kitchen was still full of the spicy smells of the cooking she had done in the afternoon. She fingered the string of onions, the few oranges that lay on the table.

'Brandy, he needs brandy.' At once, she rushed out into the street without putting on her coat.

The soldiers! She must pass them again.

They eyed her with the controlled distaste of policemen. 'I . . . I have to fetch some brandy for my husband. He's taken ill,' she blabbered in a rush of explanation, laughing like a fool.

Even at this hour of the early morning, McGuire's den was crowded and she had to elbow her way to the bar.

'Give me a bottle of Hennessy's, please. Dan's not well. I'll pay you tomorrow.'

'What manner of sickness would it be?' McGuire asked her as if he were some kind of pharmacist.

'Flu.'

'Influenza? Or is the boy under the influence?' He took down a bottle of Napoleon and began to polish it lovingly. 'I mean to say, your better half has been making light work of this stuff lately. Ever since he gave up imbibing mother's milk.'

Rosaleen clicked her tongue. 'Quit messing. I'm in a hurry.'

'Here you are, darling. Hair of the bow-wow.'

'I'll pay you tomorrow.'

'*Mañana. Mañana.*' He blew her a scornful kiss. 'Oh, I'll look forward to that! You *paying* me.'

She walked back slowly. Brendan McCartney. She remembered the stories about him. A boy from Andersonstown. Brother killed by Brits. Brendan developed a stammer afterwards, spoke less and less, turning in on himself. Stayed in his bedroom day after day, playing a trombone. Then he was interned and mistreated. Joined the Provos after his release and took up the career of hero. A most common apotheosis.

Brendan McCartney became the swaggering daredevil who escaped the Maze by dressing up in a priest's cassock and walking out the gate cool as you please. A sniper who had done away with lorryloads of Brits and policemen. Allegedly. And now . . . Paid in full. Bleached clean of those deaths by his own suicide. Final proof of sincerity.

But how could Dan possibly know him?

He doesn't know him.

'Dan does not know you. You are unknown.'

Where did they meet? Was Dan . . .? Why did he keep secrets?

She panicked suddenly. 'Secrets, secrets, secrets,' she repeated it as if to obstruct all thought.

When she returned, Dan was sitting in the same chair, staring

164

bleakly into the fire. He took the brandy and swallowed it noisily. She poured him another glassful, accidentally splashing his hand.

'I'm sorry,' she said, sitting down opposite him. 'Sorry about your friend.'

'Not my friend.'

'Oh then, you don't . . . didn't know him? Thought not, I mean, I thought you didn't have much sympathy with the Provos?'

'It's possible to be . . . you can be sorry for something and want it at the same time.'

'Tell me,' she said, moving to touch him.

He pushed her hand away. 'I'll get over it better on my own.'

'Get over what? What is there to get over?'

Dan went on drinking, sighing involuntarily every so often. She was an unwelcome spectator but could not leave.

He spoke at last: 'They ruin everything . . .' he laughed spitefully and raised his glass. 'Madmen, ruining everything . . .'

Who was he talking about? McBride? The policemen who had driven Brendan to kill himself? *Who* had ruined everything? Was he getting at her in some way?

'What do you mean?' she pleaded.

'Ha! Meaning!'

Tears were running down his face, the slow sad tears of a drunk.

She stood up and walked about the room. 'What now? What shall I do? Pace the room. Go to bed. Get up again. Tomorrow Brendan McCartney's death will be replaced by another. Tomorrow is the same day, Scarlett.'

'I'm tired,' she said to him. 'Body and soul,' she thought. 'Soul. Sole. The unalterable gap between people. Between you and me.'

'The trouble with me is I have no talents,' she said, 'only passion. Passion is not the same thing as talent, is it?'

Did he not hear?

'I have a lover.'

Not a flicker.

His thoughts were with the dead man. 'If I know you,' she thought, 'you're admiring him, his bold passing into death, his refusal to be caught. Or you're thinking that you were drinking champagne while he . . .' Were there no words that might console? She was shy. He would not let her . . . intrude.

She went to the door.

'I'm going to bed. Can I get you anything first? A freshly laundered hairshirt? Nothing? I can do nothing for you, right? Goodnight . . . Sleep uptight.' She closed the door softly.

# 18

'Dan . . . Dan . . .'

The pillow beside her was smooth.

'Where are you? What time?' Six a.m. Had he sat up all night? 'Oh, you fool, you idiot.'

She pulled on her clothes and crept downstairs, picturing him by the fireside, sunk in sorrow, exactly as she had left him last night. Not there!

He must have gone to work. So early?

No, he has gone for a walk, reckoning to be back in time before you wake.

She made tea and prepared a feed for Louis, whom she woke deliberately, something she had never done before.

'All right for some, isn't it?' she muttered to him. 'Just walk out when they feel like it.' The baby made gurgling sounds of agreement.

At nine o'clock she rang the hospital.

'Could I speak to Daniel Keenan please?'

'Ward?'

'Oh, I'm sorry, I don't know.'

'Are you a relative?'

'No. I mean yes. I'm his wife.'

'What manner of ailment has he?'

'He's not a patient. He's a final year medic. On some kind of women's surgical . . .' She was transferred from voice to voice.

Finally, the correct Ward Sister.

'He's not here, dear. We're not expecting him. Sure, it's his day off.'

'Oh, of course. How stupid of me to forget . . .'

'Is anything wrong?'

'No. Oh no. Sorry to bother you.'

She replaced the receiver. What an imbecile she was!

167

'Are you a relative? . . . No, I'm his wife! . . . It's his day off . . . Oh yes, of course, silly me!'

He had been strange last night. What if . . .? Some kind of nervous collapse? You shouldn't have left him . . .

But ever since she had known him, he had frightened her at times with his sudden fits of bleakness, his queer emptiness of vision. There were days when he would come home and flop down on the bed fully dressed, not even his shoes removed, and would not utter a single word. Other times he would drink a whole bottle of gin in a matter of hours, shunning all company. How she hated that, when he swallowed drink after drink with an air of grim dedication . . . And then the aftermath of vomiting and remorse. It always happened after a patient's death. His protest.

All day she waited, attending to nothing but the repeated feedings and changings of the child. She could take no comfort from him. Today the baby seemed little more than a flow of food and excrement. Sometimes she used to fool herself that his unshrinking gaze meant he could fathom her thoughts. But today she knew that it wasn't because he knew so much that he could look at her that way. It was because he knew so little. As he grew older, he would stop looking people in the eye.

In the late evening a storm arose. Rosaleen sat listening to the groaning wind, trying not to be a coward. It was the sort of night when she and Dan would be unable to sleep, and would lie talking together. If Dan were here . . . She ascended to their room and opened the window to lean out. Her hair and the upper part of her body became soaked with rain, as she watched the sky and listened. 'When I was a child,' she told him, 'I used to fancy I heard voices talking in the wind, crying for help, or for attention . . . forlorn voices . . .'

He did not come home.

In the dawn light she began searching round the house, scanning for clues. The suit he had worn to the party was back hanging in the wardrobe in the baby's room. She checked the pockets of all his jackets and trousers. A bus ticket, some coins, nothing. As she stood inhaling his faint familiar smell, she spied some fallen garments on the wardrobe floor and stooped to lift them.

A pair of jeans, torn and stiff with mud. How unlike Dan to stash away something like that. She fished out a sweater and something thudded on to the floor. Money! Money hidden . . . was it hidden? . . . inside the sweater. A bundle of neat dirty fivers.

Rosaleen was calm. Her brain seemed to slow down.

It was all right. Of course Dan had money. They had money. He had told her about it. This was their money for getting out. A loan from his wealthy Aunt Leah. But surely she would have given him a cheque! Well, not necessarily.

She remembered the few things Dan had told her about the woman. A solitary, a lover of her own company, a rich woman who lived in a pretence of poverty, even taking to her bed on cold days to save on heating fuel. Yes, such a perverse old woman might shun banks. But then, it was hard to imagine her ever parting with her money, even for a temporary loan! Especially to an indifferent and unapproved nephew, by his own account. And if she had lent it to him, she would never have sent such a stack of fivers through the post. He must have gone to see her. A day's journey. When? There was that time a few weeks ago when he had not come home at all and had turned up at lunchtime the following day. His eyes weary and hooded, hair all damp and plastered.

Swore blind he had helped in a casualty and had fallen asleep exhausted in a side ward at the hospital. 'For Godsake, Rosaleen, don't you trust me?' he had asked her.

Why would he deceive her over that? A harmless fund-raising trip to a cranky old aunt.

'No. You've never been near your aunt.'

Rosaleen counted the notes, arranging them in heaps around her. £450. She stood up with sudden energy, knowing that she must find Dan at once, sort things out.

Buoyant for a few moments, she began to prepare for going out. But it all took so long. Changing Louis, finding his clothes, manoeuvring his limbs into them, fiddling with the countless maddening buttons . . . She began to cry in a quiet resigned way.

It was after ten o'clock when she left and headed for Marty's house. Mrs Boyle answered the door.

'Is Marty here?'

'No, love. Sure, she's gone to school. Sometimes she manages to rouse herself to go!'

'Oh well, I was going to ask her to mind Louis for me, but it doesn't matter.'

169

'Come on in. My two daughters-in-law are here. We'll mind him for you.'

'Oh, thanks very much!'

'Not at all! There's so many kids in here, one more won't notice.'

The tiny sitting room was an obstacle course of children and toys. The mothers had managed to commandeer the sofa.

They were two women in their late twenties, one a pallid spiritless type who was sucking fiercely on a cigarette. 'This is Ellie.' The other was a raven-haired fleshy woman of brash good looks. 'And this is our Isabel, Nick's wife.'

Isabel gave Rosaleen a welcoming look and snatched Louis from her.

'What have we here?'

'He's a boy. Seven months.'

'Oh, I'd love a boy! Aren't you a gorgeous wee article?'

Rosaleen noticed that all the children in the room were girls, all uniformly beautiful, with burnished brown hair.

'Yes,' Ellie agreed. 'We do a strong line in girls in our family.'

'You must adore him?' Isabel asked Rosaleen with an air of subtle accusation.

'Oh yes, of course, I adore him.'

None of the children seemed to overhear their mothers' disappointment at their gender.

Mrs Boyle spoke to Rosaleen. 'You've time for a drop of tea?'

'No, not really.'

'Sure you have. You're not getting out till you're fed and watered.'

'Fed and drowned, more like, the rate we go through the tea!'

The other two women gossiped languidly together, making private allusions. A solemn little girl approached Rosaleen and handed over her doll for inspection. Rosaleen looked into the doll's paralysed blue stare, toyed with the manipulable limbs, noticed the inaccurately sculpted hole through which the doll could urinate clean water. 'A doll that weeps and pees!' she thought. 'I'll invent a doll that can spit.'

'She's lovely. What's her name?'

'Got no name.'

'Where are you off to?' Mrs Boyle asked after serving steaming cups of tea and passing round a heaped plateful of cakes.

'Oh, I don't know . . . I mean, I have to find Dan.'

170

'Have you mislaid him?' Isobel said, her face full of innocent mockery.

'There are a few places he could be.'

'What's the emergency?'

'Nothing. He's been away. Working. I have to see him about something.'

Her face was hot, even her eyes were hot.

She saw Isobel and Mrs Boyle exchange sly looks.

'How long has he been away?'

'Oh, just since early this morning,' she lied.

Isobel relaxed back into the sofa. Daylight absences of husbands were no matter of concern. She nuzzled Louis and then held his head against her breasts. Rosaleen tried to look away from the glaring white tops of those breasts exposed by the skimpy sweater.

'Look, love,' Isobel said. 'He's gone off in a huff, am I right? Don't chase after him. You must never let them know they've got you worried . . . Oh dear,' she laughed, 'do I detect a certain tension?' She reached for a cigarette. Her lighter failed to ignite. 'Damn, hell, shit . . .'

At last it worked and she breathed in deeply.

'Don't smoke while you're holding my baby,' Rosaleen thought, eyeing the woman, the full length of her self-satisfied body, the soft plump legs, the slight inflation of flesh over the stomach.

'Is it wise to smoke?'

A pause.

'OK, so we know you're married to a wee medical student!'

'I mean, in pregnancy . . .'

'I am not pregnant! Who said I was pregnant? Godsake!' She was blustering like someone charged with a criminal offence.

Mrs Boyle spoke first: 'Oh Jesus, Bel, maybe . . . that might be . . . you were so sick this morning.'

Isobel sat still for a few moments, her mouth a damp line of consternation which transformed suddenly into a luxurious smile. 'Just can't keep that man away from me!' She looked at Rosaleen with obvious gloating dislike.

'Oh, Bel,' Mrs Boyle scolded.

'It's not my fault she has to run after her husband!'

Rosaleen stood, addressed herself in a formal manner to Mrs Boyle: 'Thank you for the tea. And for minding Louis. I won't be long.'

Isobel's explosion of laughter followed her into the street.

Running after my husband . . . True. Right. And she *was* at his mercy, that was true as well. But she could not go back and wait meekly for him to remember he had a home. For him to drop in at prison-visiting time . . . Besides, what if something dreadful had happened, was happening? She walked past the newsagents', the advertisement for *Cosmopolitan*: 'Sex, the next growth area . . .'

'Erin Pizzey tells you what you can learn from rejection.'

'Be his lover, not his mother!'

The army helicopter droned above her. It was always there, so ceaselessly there, that she often forgot to hear it.

Englishmen in the sky, watching. God's eyes. Angels on long shifts. Everyone is looking for something, someone, just as I am looking now for you. Why did God create the world? Could it be that God . . . Out of boredom? . . . Out of desire? Increase and multiply. Go forth and populate the earth. We do. The earth is populated. And still we are alone. Over a hundred million sperm in the ejaculation of the human male. And still alone . . . Even if I find you, I will be alone.

Inventory of places searched: her parents' house. McGuire's pub. Every other pub in the vicinity, ten in all. The hospital staff common room and canteen. The university bookshop, bar, grounds . . .

She went home to listen to the news. No dumped bodies, no abductions. Wherever he had gone, he had chosen to go.

She went to meet Marty on her way home from school.

'Hi, stranger.'

'Hey, Marty, do me a favour?'

'Depends.'

'I left Louis in your house. Would you bring him back for me?'

'No, I will not! You crippled or what?'

'Please Marty. It's only a few yards.'

'Why not get him yourself then?'

'OK. Next time you want something off me, forget it!'

'What would I ever want off you?' she said nastily, before relenting. 'Oh, OK, I'll bring him to you, just so long as you remember, I fetched you your baby, right?'

'Right.'

She appeared a few minutes later in Rosaleen's kitchen.

172

'Here you are, one spoilt stuffed infant! . . . Rosaleen, have you fallen out with Dan?'

'Your sister-in-law is one big-mouthed bitch!'

'She was good enough to look after your kid!' Marty snapped back, then laughed. 'You didn't half put the wind up her! With your diagnosis.'

'She is, isn't she?'

Marty shrugged. 'She'll blame you if she is! The evil eye . . . Where's Dan?'

'Not at home.'

'Oh, Monsieur is not at home . . . What is that supposed to mean?'

'I don't know where he is.'

'I'm never going to get married.'

'OK, so don't get married! Congratulations!'

'Keep your hair on. Do you want me to stay here . . . until he comes back?'

'No. No, thanks.'

'I'll maybe look in on you tomorrow.'

'Good.'

'It'll be OK, Rosaleen.'

Marty left. Not a sound in the house. Straining, Rosaleen could just manage to hear the helicopter.

'Our Father, which art in Heaven . . .

'Hollow be thy name . . .

'I have looked for you all day without finding you . . . Where are you?

'Come soon, O Englishman, come soon . . .'

## 19

He cursed his ill luck that Frost had picked on him. Today of all days. Not that he could imagine a day when a clash with Frost would be convenient. 'Clash' being the wrong word. Too combative. Suggested he was in with a chance. He was really like a worm enduring the attentions of an evil bored schoolboy. The only hope was that Frosty would find some more attractive project, a big bomb or some cheeky dereliction of duty which required his talent for retribution. Unlikely. He remembered how Frost had ogled him.

Gerry was restless, charged with energy he did not know how to use. Last night he had seen Dan. Spoken to him. Exchanged words. Social event of the year.

He was shocked out of his skin to see Dan walking into the guardroom. Well, walking with assistance, as it were. Somewhat the worse for wear and tear. A bruise over the left eye. So he had been 'encouraged' to pay them a visit. 'Fell down' in official parlance. The Irish were always keeling over, according to army medical reports. Natural inclination to the horizontal. It turned out that Dan was spotted entering a house which was under surveillance. A possible HQ or hideaway for a cell operating in another district. He emerged half an hour later. Soldiers bundled him pronto into their unmarked car. Dan was obviously at the fuzzy regret stage of a drinking spree. He kept blinking and sighing. Gerry remembered the last time he had seen him close to. The time he had twisted his arm and made him spreadeagle against the pub wall. Rosaleen's wild white face as she shouted 'Leave him alone.'

'This is the man my Rosaleen loves,' he thought. 'He knows everything about her.' Gerry had an impulse to touch him.

He said shyly: 'Shall I get you a glass of water?'

Dan looked through him.

'Fuck you! I'm not a waiter!' Gerry thought.

Pike entered, his face afire with wanting to crack this one double-quick.

'Where's the comedian?' he said to no one in particular before heaving himself into the chair on the opposite side of the table from Dan. 'Blotted our copybook, haven't we? Slipped from grace?' His voice turned thick. 'Right, you, you can answer me straight and be home tucked up in bed before breakfast. Otherwise, I hope you have a lot of time on your hands.'

Dan cleared his throat three times.

'Why did you go to seventeen Ardagh Street?'

'Just to see someone.'

'Aye, right. Why would you be wanting to see Conor Delaney.' No answer.

'Friend of yours?'

'No. Not particularly.'

'So you went on business.'

'No.'

'Were you summoned there for some reason? An offer you couldn't refuse?'

'No.'

'If it wasn't social and it wasn't business and you weren't sent for, why did you go?'

Silence.

'I don't think much of the company you keep.'

'It's preferable to yours!' Dan burst out.

'No, no,' Gerry told him inwardly. 'Not like that. Mistake.'

'What do you do for the Provos?'

'Nothing.'

Pike leaned back, spread his hands. 'Consider this. You're not going to be popular. You pay them a social call, right? Walk out straight into our arms. Won't they wonder about that?'

'They don't like me anyway.'

'Who doesn't like you' Pike injected carelessness into his voice, but Dan saw the trap at last. It was obvious to Gerry that Dan was not mixed up with the Provos. He would have been better trained, alert to the ruses behind questions.

'Did it feel good hobnobbing with the big time? Not so hot now, is it? . . . On your own . . . Your mates won't give a shit what happens to you. Neither do I. Come on, you and I both know you're small fry. Pathetic. You're not in the McCartney class, you know. Rather die than divulge. So don't waste my time.'

Gerry noticed Dan give a start at McCartney's name, as if Pike had hit accidentally on what was on his mind. Tears started to stream down his face. Pike stood up, grimaced at Gerry. 'Another blubber! Let him stew for a while. I'm going for a bite.'

Dan mopped his face. 'Can I have some aspirin, please?' His voice was husky but with a tinge of petulance.

Gerry stuck his head round the door, yelled for tea and aspirins. 'Thanks.'

Gerry spoke: 'That guy McCartney. Desperate way to kill himself, hanging.'

He thought Dan would snub him, suspect him of being on the interrogation rota.

'They didn't supply him with a variety of means!'

'Did you know him?' Gerry said suddenly, convinced that he had guessed right. He raised his hand. 'OK, don't answer . . .'

The tea was brought in and some aspirin dissolved in water. Dan inspected it, smelt it, then gulped it down.

'When my friend killed himself,' Gerry said, 'I went berserk. Ran straight to his bed and stole his things, fags, money, everything . . . Do you understand that?'

'It was no use to him, I suppose,' Dan said indifferently.

'I didn't want his damned things! I wanted to do something . . . against him!' ('My mates don't count, of course, of course, only your precious mates!')

'Won't your wife worry when you don't turn up?' he said sternly. 'How long will I be held?'

'Depends when you decide to cough up. Rather you than me.'

Dan's wretched face made him contrite. He knew that Dan was just a talker, a big ideas merchant. What was the point of the glued-lip routine? It provoked Pike. He was like some crazed gold-digger who refused to believe that there was no gold to be extracted. Everything Dan knew, or thought he knew, or could be prevailed upon to remember, everything would be drawn out of him like slow pus.

'Look, I don't think you're in the IRA. Make it easy. Clear up what you were doing in that house. He'll get it out of you anyway, I promise.'

'No, I'm not a member of the . . . Oh no, they only take the cream! They only want the most courageous, most committed . . .'

'Steady on! I know all that. I couldn't be killed by a better class of person! God, I wish the selection had been so fussy when I visited my local army recruitment office!'

That shut him up. He had hit home. So the idiot had been offering himself to the Provos!

'I'm going to take Rosaleen away from you,' Gerry vowed silently. Since then he had been inflamed by the thought of her alone. He guessed that Dan would hold out on his interrogators. The disgrace of having nothing much to confess would make him tease them and they would pay him back by detaining him for the full seventy-two hours. Maybe. Rosaleen was alone. And he was alone. Two streets between them. A million miles. He had been granted an off-duty pass for the evening. He kept announcing to everyone that he was going to Lisburn. He had no clear plan. If he could only catch a glimpse of her.

In less than one hour he cleaned and polished everything brutally. He laid his kit out with supernatural neatness over the bed.


Gerry stood still as a waxwork while Frost inspected his kit. He was sure that Frost could find no fault. Still his nerves were screwed tight. He waited for the denunciation. Frost was full of menace, gliding his lizard's stare back and forth over everything. Gerry wanted to do something scandalous, like suddenly to grab the Captain and spin him round in a waltz, shouting some serenade. Or preferably knock the bugger down. Dance on his grave. On his grave face. He glanced swiftly out at the sky. 'Soon, soon, I'll be outside.'

'H'mm,' said Frost, betraying neither satisfaction nor displeasure. 'Open that cupboard.'

Gerry hesitated for the fraction of a moment.

'Don't fret. I won't wreck your embroidery.'

He held his breath, praying that Frost would content himself with admiring the symmetrical arrangement of his few possessions. But no, he began to delve into everything!

If Gerry could only wrench those interfering paws out of it. 'Keep your famous laying on of hands for your bombs, like you're paid to!' he thought. It was so bloody unfair and Frost must know it! 'Bull' was relaxed in Belfast. A degree of scruffiness was tolerated by all the officers. There were rarely dress inspections, and never this kind of prying into a soldier's personal possessions. Unless he was suspected of being a thief or a junkie.

Frost was flicking through his letters, tossing them on to the bed as if he were dealing cards. Then the books, more slowly. 'Lawrence,' he said it with disgust. 'Gide . . . Wasn't he a homosexual?'

'He was a brilliant writer, Sir.'

'*The Immoralist*! Very apt!'

Frost looked gratefully for a few moments at the next title. Some pink appeared in his yellow cheeks. It was *British Army Atrocities in Northern Ireland*. The Gorgon Medusa could not have rivalled the gaze which he trained on Gerry. 'What a fascinating library.'

'It's not mine, Sir . . . the pamphlet, I mean, Sir. It belonged to Private Sinclair, who passed away, Sir. In the shooting accident, Sir.'

'Left it to you in his will, I expect?'

'It came into my possession, Sir. I was intending to get rid of it. I thought it would be best. Discreet, like. I didn't want Des . . . I didn't want Sinclair to be misunderstood. He took an interest in Irish history, you see . . . the political background and that. He liked to keep acquainted with the views, I mean, the allegations . . .'

'Of the victims?' Frost interrupted.

Gerry said nothing.

'This chap, Sinclair. The late lamented historian. What were his views on the subject?'

'I don't really know, sir.'

'You were *friends*, were you not?'

'Yessir.'

'Spent time together? On duty? Off duty? Sometimes alone, just the two of you?'

'Yessir.'

'And there was no occasion when you were sequestered together, you two good *friends*, sharing little worries and intimacies, no occasion when Private Sinclair voiced an opinion to you on the conduct of his colleagues in the Emerald Isle?'

'We mentioned it once or twice. In general terms, Sir.'

Gerry was shaking with physical anguish at this talk about Des. It was the first time his name had been mentioned since the death.

'How many British Army atrocities have been committed in this country?'

'None, Sir.'

'How many?'

'None whatsoever, Sir.'

'One night, an Argyll patrol was staking out a farmhouse in Fermanagh. They entered a barn and encountered the owner and a farmhand. Questioned them. The civilians had no known connection with paramilitaries. They were unarmed. No doubt they were some-what surly but they offered no violence or threat. They ended up impaled on their own pitchforks. Are you familiar with the case?'

'Yessir.'

'What do you think of the sergeant's action?'

'An aberration, Sir.'

'That's your unexaggerated opinion? Aren't you being somewhat fanatically partisan?'

'Rotten apples, Sir,' Gerry said desperately, his eyes downcast.

'I call them cold-blooded murderers.'

Gerry let out a sigh of relief, searching Frost's face, suspecting a trap. 'That's what I think,' he said, then clammed up.

Frost lashed his hand across Gerry's face, making him stagger. 'I would have thought that a man who favours French novelists and political discussions would have set great store on speaking his own mind,' he said quietly.

'Right! No more prevarication. The truth, man, not what you imagine I expect to hear. You're not bright enough to figure that out!'

'How can I? How can I say what I feel!'

'Spare me your precious feelings. Say what you *think*.'

'OK! There are atrocities . . . and cover-ups. We're as bad as them! That's what I think.'

The voice turned gentle. 'You're in great danger, you know. You have doubts, a superfine conscience, you're impressionable. I'll tell you something. I have never come across a Provisional fighter who was troubled by a doubt or the ghost of a doubt. If you come up against one of the local heroes, you won't stand a chance. Do you know how a snake operates? He paralyses his prey with a squirt of venom. Watches it writhe. Moves in for the final kill at his leisure. Who gave you that pamphlet?'

'I don't know where it came from, Sir.'

'I see.' The Captain sighed and resumed his diligent investigation of Gerry's things. His Belfast photographs. Oh Christ, he had forgotten to hide that picture of Rosaleen!

'Who is this?'

'Girlfriend in England, Sir.'

'This is not English.'

179

'Yessir. Hundred per cent, Sir. As far as I know, Sir.'

'I know that look. Mixture of loathing and fear. Overdose of sulkiness. A Belfast face. She gave you the pamphlet, did she not?'

'No, Sir. Never spoke to her in my life, Sir.'

'Incitement to disaffection is a criminal offence.'

'I swear, I just liked the look of her, so I took the picture from the files.'

'Economizing on girlie magazines?'

'For Godsake! Oh, don't, don't harm her!'

Frost moved closer and touched his shoulder gently. 'Unwise attachments will be the ruin of you, my lad.'

Gerry weakened totally. He could not look up or speak.

Frost stepped back, assumed his down-to-business voice: 'Straighten! I am taking this photograph to run a security check. Crown property, in any case, as you freely admitted. Report to my office tomorrow at 8.00 hours.'

And he was gone. At last, he was gone. Gerry sank to the bed and sobbed. He realized that Frost had pulled the old interrogator's trick. They start off hard, cruel, unpredictably violent. Then without warning, they turn nice, talk warmly, offer you tea or cigarettes . . . It felt real, maybe it was real, a tenderness for the prey. Anyway, it was the nice part of the act that broke you up. He went over and over the interview, sifting every word, exclaiming out loud as he saw how crawling and cheap his behaviour was. *He* was. He had betrayed Rosaleen. Des. Himself. Especially himself. How could he go on without a shred of dignity? A dog was better off than he was.

He reached blindly to reassemble his things. *The Immoralist* fell open and he glanced at the prefacing quotation from Psalms: 'I will praise Thee, for I am fearfully and wonderfully made.'

'I am fearfully and wonderfully made,' he sneered to himself. 'I am made wonderfully fearful . . . What am I going to do? What can I do?' The memory came to him of a crazed old man in Cromac Street ramming his head time after time against a wall. Gerry went over to the mirror and studied his reflection. He looked as if he was waiting for a command. By God, he *was* waiting for a command! His face was dull, his body hard, smooth, poised to . . . demolish.

He had to sit down. Think. Frost had told him. Think. Spare me your precious feelings. What had turned him into a slavish creep? Oh, he knew, he knew rightly. He had just never formulated it. Or faced it. He would rather dream about Rosaleen. But he knew. Why he slobbed around on his offs, feeble and empty. Why he had developed an appetite for raids, patrols, arrests. Because it was impossible to act for himself. He had to crush the instinct to act for himself and only do what he was told. So his need for orders had mounted up. Even though every single order made a hard pellet of hatred within him . . . No wonder Frost had flummoxed him. Changing the tune out of the blue like that. All of a sudden he was supposed to have opinions! Oh, why the hell had he joined? Because Des . . . Well, why had Des joined? Maybe he had grown tired of being just a street hero. Fancied some real danger. Des had believed in the power of his body. In personal valiance. Maybe heroes didn't even want an audience, the worship of inferior beings. What had Des wanted? And what did Frost get out of his daily death-dodging? They needed to be indes-tructible. To keep proving it. At least Frost did. Des had bitten off more than he could swallow. Well, you made it, you bastard. Well and truly unassailable now. Unavailable. Like Rosaleen.

He winced at the thought of Frost looking at her phtotgraph, discovering her identity, age, income, connections; making assump-tions about her beliefs, her capacity for damage. As if she was just anybody. Nobody. I am in love with nobody. No crime.

Tomorrow Frost would grill him about her. No, it was unbearable. Gerry looked again at his pathetic heap of belongings. Now he had nothing. Not even a secret.

He sloughed off his uniform, surveyed his naked body in the mirror. 'I am fearfully and wonderfully made.' He felt cleaner with-out the uniform. His facial muscles relaxed. He tried to ease his whole frame. Could be mistaken for a human being. Yes, he didn't look too bad. He went quickly to remove his fancy togs from his suitcase under the bed. Blue woollen sweater, silk shirt, dark grey Donegal tweed suit, Italian leather shoes. Bought in Belfast one extravagant day with his hoarded wages to ward off misery but never yet worn. A costume for a different lifestyle. My life has no style. Even that's wrong. It could hardly be called *my* life. His mood became rapt and attentive as he put on the beautiful clothes. He wanted to be outside, out there. To have a house no one dared enter without invitation. To feed, drink, make love, and be left in peace. To walk out free to meet her, her face, her voice, her body. He wanted to be full and glutted with natural happiness.

## 20

She did not report him missing. He did not come home. No one came. If she went to the police . . . no, she could not. Suppose he was involved with the IRA . . . Voluntarily or against his will? It didn't matter. She would place him in worse danger by going to the police. Danger from the Provos or danger from the army . . . Once or twice she prepared to go out but turned back at the door. There was really nowhere to go.

When her own food was used up, she started eating baby foods, puréed vegetables and desserts. The pedal bin was full of empty tins with fat grinning babies' faces looking up at her. Smile, smile, smile.

She imagined Dan on a ship. Running away from her. Or staying quietly somewhere locally, going to work as usual. Putting on his stiff white coat and his hard passive face, walking round with consultants on galloping visits from bed to bed.

'I'm not a purveyor of happiness,' he had said to her. He had promised. 'You didn't lie . . . Lying on a slab? Are you dead?'

The meat department, that's what he called the mortuary. 'You should never have called it that . . .'

'If you're not dead, why don't you come and see me?'

He would say she held death wishes towards him. 'You killed me in your mind,' he would say. 'It's true that I hate you. I remember the taste of your skin and I hate you.'

Every night she lay fully dressed on top of the bed.

The bed of passion. Bed of ration.

The weather remained stormy. She seemed to be always thinking of nothing, just listening to wind and rain. It frightened her. Although it was nonsense to think that weather meant anything, echoed anything. But she remembered the story of Cromwell's death. While he took his time over it, an unusual tempest raged outside. She recalled the words from her history textbook: 'When Satan reclaimed him,

Nature gave a vast groan at his removal.' And at the Crucifixion, the sky darkened over . . .

On the fourth day she ventured out of the house, leaving the baby asleep. The street was deserted. Her footsteps rang out eerily. She reached the corner shop. Closed! What was going on? Her fists were hammering on the door, beating against her frowning reflection. She didn't want anything, but she must get in.

'Hey! What's the racket?'

She was surrounded by four soldiers.

'I . . . the shop is closed.'

'Sunday, innit? . . . Why ain't you down the church with the rest of 'em?'

She glanced bewildered from face to face.

'Maybe she's a heretic.'

'Maybe she's a bad girl,' the nearest one said.

Acne ran wild on his face. He was leering at her like a deadly adolescent who practised his menace in a mirror.

'Excuse me,' she said, but he barred her way.

He clamped his hands on her breasts. She gasped but willed her eyes dry and steady.

'Missing him, are you? . . . Need anything doing? . . . Round the house, like?'

The others laughed, a hot furtive laughter.

'Don't speak much, do it?'

'Maybe it prefers action.'

The groper moved one hand to cup her chin, the other to encircle her throat. He pushed her head back. His spots, his teeth, his lips, hovered near her face.

'Listen, Irish,' he hissed in her ear, 'I'm going to suck your cunt so hard your head will shrink between your shoulders . . . With this, see . . .' he shoved his tongue into her ear with a grunting sound.

She closed her eyes to shut out those three watching faces. What would happen? Would they . . .? In daylight? Were they queuing? Brits in one of their polite queues? Jesus, send someone round the corner . . . make them stop . . .

He was pressing his fat thing against her. His breathing became thick and wavy in her ear. 'Tough shit, tough shit,' he kept mumbling. No! Touch it! He was telling her to touch it! Vomit came into her mouth and erupted, spattering his sleeve with slimy streaks. He sprang back, red-faced and cursing: 'Mucky Irish tart!'

The others jeered at him. 'You make them come at the wrong end . . .'

Still choking, she shot past them and ran to the house, almost fainting while she tried to fit the key into the lock. But no boots were coming after her.

She ran to the kitchen sink but could not be sick again. She wanted to throw up everything. To be dry and empty inside. She retched and spat at the thought of those men. The way they had looked at her. Without heat, without mercy, without even much curiosity. What might they have done? What might they still do?

She moaned at the sudden thought of their different sweats mingling on her skin. They knew she was alone. They could come anytime. Break in if she refused to open the door. They were the law.

'You see what you have left me to, Dan!' It was his fault. Obviously, she was up for grabs.

Crying, she went into the room where the Crucifix was hanging. The King of the Jews. He knew the meaning of humiliation. His body was abused. The first nude pin-up.

Oh no, Jesus was no use to her! What was the point of God taking on the mantle of humanity if he only tried it as a man?

The baby started to cry and she hurried to see him. Soaked, of course. She stripped off his nappy, applied cream to the child's behind and pale damp penis. 'God, touch it! Touch it, the soldier said!' An uncontrollable sob that sounded like a laugh came out of her. 'My hands are magic,' she said out loud. 'They turn things to dust. That would have pleased him, wouldn't it?' The baby gave a delighted cry. Would he grow up and use his sex as a weapon? No, it must not be so!

She went to the mirror. 'I know that you are me,' she thought. 'What is it about you?'

She was dressed in faded jeans and an ancient sweater. Hardly aphrodisiac. No cosmetics. No 'fuck me' face. Maybe she looked too soft and smooth and undefined? Not a real person. Just a source of sensation, an accessory. Gentlemen prefer blands. She shrugged. Maybe it was nothing to do with her looks. Men always thought that women were just dying to be jumped on. She remembered seeing *Last Tango in Paris* in the university film club. Marlon Brando with his budding paunch and dirty raincoat just walks up to a stranger inspecting a flat for rent. Sticks it in her without preamble, and, of course, she loves it. Rolls on the floor in appreciation. His slave. His instrument. Then there's the scene where he greases her buttocks with butter like some roasting turkey. Fucks her hurtfully in the rear, all the while spewing out his hatred of life. Empties himself in a hole. 'I'm not a hole,' Rosaleen told herself, turning away from the mirror, suddenly troubled by the unbidden memory of Gerry. Hadn't he just walked up to *her*, ready for action? Gerry in the cemetery, the gravestones around them like shields. Gerry in the factory, the snaky slither of his belt as he removed it . . .

She resolved not to go outside the house again. There was only enough baby food for Louis for one more day. Apart from that, there was a packet of sugar and a bottle of champagne left over from Katrina's engagement party. Rosaleen lit the fire, intending to stay up all night. They might take her, but they would never take her by surprise. She listened dreamily to the radio for a while, gradually realizing that she was hungry. Why not phone one of the posh foodstores downtown tomorrow? Get them to deliver? 'Now that I'm a woman of means. Of ill-gotten gains.' But no, they would never send one of their precious vans into the area. They would think it was a ruse, a hijack plan.

Rosaleen fetched the sugar and the champagne from the kitchen. Ate spoonfuls of the sugar, spilling some on the floor. She uncorked the champagne, saddened by the festive little explosion. Drinking alone was Dan's vice.

'Just keeping the tradition alive, Daniel!'

She sat by the fire drinking steadily. Her skin was glowing. All her internal organs seemed to unclench. Grains of sugar were everywhere, sticking to her fingers and the soles of her feet. She licked thoroughly between each finger, bathed her feet with handfuls of champagne. Sham pain. She wondered if Dan would ever kill himself. He often swore he would die rather than endure certain circumstances. Illness, disablement, other unspecified ordeals. He had access to despatch. He could get the necessary pills. Knew the lethal doses. But she remembered something else he had told her. Once, on a flight to the States, he had sat in a lather of sweat throughout the entire trip, hands gripping the armrests, unable to say a single word.

'Where are you, Dan? Are you bluffing?'

She began to strip, enjoying her flesh warm and luxurious in the firelight. The booze, the hunger, the heat, the tiredness were all mixing to make her feel intensely real and yet unearthly.

The baby woke crying softly. Rosaleen went and fetched him from the carry cot, sat down by the fire again with him snuggled against her stomach. He quietened and fell asleep again. She knew it was the contact with her soft warm skin that had lulled him and she felt a surge of comfort and power. She knew for certain that Dan was wrong to talk so coolly of self-destruction; a medic devoted to the saving of life who toted around his private bottle of get-out pills!

All men were wrong who held bodies in cheap esteem. Pornographers. Politicians. Armies. Even priests.

Health of the soul does not depend on mortification of the body. Mortification. *Mors*, *mortis*. Death. Putting the flesh to death. 'No wonder we have such crooked penitent ways of loving each other!' she thought. She was never going to hate herself again because there were men who wanted to abuse her.

But everyone was part of the conspiracy. She decided once and for all to cut out her own lingering instinctive loyalty to the Provisionals. Earlier today after she was molested, she had kept thinking of the Provos, craving their protection, wanting their vengeance on her attackers. But there was nothing to choose between armies. The Provisionals were well-named. Hadn't they succeeded in making life even more provisional and uncertain than it need be?

She laid the child down and went over to the window in an odd rapt state, her palms placed beneath her breasts. A bird landed unsteadily on the ledge outside.

'If Dan were here, he would name what sort of bird you are, explain all about your auditory system, mating habits, hating habits . . .'

A man passing by on the opposite side of the street caught sight of her and stopped in his tracks. He stared, mouth gaping.

Rosaleen closed her eyes to banish him. 'Oh, go away, stupid man. I'll do what I like in the privacy of my own window!'

Minutes later, he was still there.

'Don't you understand? Don't any of you understand? Why are you so desperate? It's not . . . chic!'

## 21

Her house was fifteenth from the north end of the street, twelfth from the far end. The back doors were indistinguishable. What if he made a mistake? He counted. Recounted. He moved forward suddenly. Now or never. Pressed down the latch, slipped into the backyard, dropped into a crouching position beside the rubbish bin. His shoes were in a puddle. Damn it! No sound from the house. He edged forward to the window. Yes! She was there. Alone. Stooping to light a cigarette from the gas ring of the cooker, holding back her hair from the flame. Then she stood there, her strong brooding face in profile. She was wearing a nightdress, despite the earliness of the evening. For a moment he wanted to run away from her. But then his fingers were tapping the window.

It took her several moments to recover and to recognize him. At last she unlocked the door, guided him past her and rebolted the door without a word. He went ahead of her into the living room, where she hovered in the centre of the floor, glancing around as if the room had become strange and uncomfortable to her.

There were sharp creases round her mouth. 'Is this Rosaleen? My Rosaleen?'

'You look tired,' he said, meaning to show concern but it came out like disappointment.

'It's chilly in here,' she said, bending down to rekindle the fire.

'Oh, I don't mind,' he told her, but she ignored him. Her hair parted down her back in two even strands. He wanted to stroke it.

The fire would not light. It was a hopeless effort but she would not give up, and her patient hospitable gestures filled him with a bitter compassion. Or maybe it was the room which aroused such feelings in him, with its shabby furniture, bare lightbulb, mingled smells of disinfectant and talcum powder. When his eyes grew accustomed to the leaden light, he noticed that the baby was lying asleep in a carrycot in the corner, two sticky rivulets of chocolate smearing the sides of its mouth. The child's presence irritated him, as if it would hear and understand and condemn everything.

'Please get up,' he said. 'Why is the kid sleeping downstairs?'

'I keep an eye on him. I worry about . . . cot death. And . . . I worry about lots of things.'

'You're not ill, I hope? You're undressed, I mean, you're dressed for bed . . .'

'That's me, I'm afraid, early to bed, late to rise . . .' The joke fell flatter than Gerry's optimism. She cleared her throat.

His famous silk shirt was glued to his back with sweat, despite the cold air. The suit was a big mistake. He realized he must have lost weight and it didn't fit him. She would probably think he had borrowed it. Trying to look like something to write home about.

'We haven't had much practice,' he said, 'at conversation.'

'Oh, words, words,' she said inexplicably.

He touched her lightly on the arm and she bridled so violently it alarmed him.

'Don't!' she yelled. 'For Christ's sake! Can't you see? I am *not* the sort of person who can be *touched*!'

'I didn't mean . . .'

The baby whimpered, drawing her attention. He settled again.

'He won't waken,' she said more calmly. 'I gave him an aspirin to make him sleep . . . Oh, my husband would go mad if he found out . . . By the way, my husband will be here any minute. He's already late.'

'Three days late.'

'Oh, my God.' She covered her eyes with her hands.

'Your husband's OK,' Gerry heard himself saying. 'The Special Branch are holding him. Don't . . . It's nothing, routine stuff.'

She had risen, suddenly full of blind energy. 'I have to go. Oh God, my clothes . . . I need my clothes . . . Get out of here, you!'

'No, wait.'

'It's you, isn't it? You've gotten rid of him!'

'No, I swear . . . Don't go. They'll only insult you . . . Believe me, he is all right . . . Basically. And he'll be released soon . . . soon. What's that?' he asked startled by a sound.

'Rain,' she whispered, as if she could hardly speak.

'She loves him,' he thought bitterly.

'He brought it on himself, you know . . . Maybe he's enjoying it.'

188

'You don't know him. You don't know what you're talking about.'

'I spoke to him. He wasn't half so bothered about you as you are about him!'

She turned away like someone struck in the face. He followed her and pulled her into his arms. 'Sorry. I'm sorry. I didn't mean to tell you where he is. I wanted you to think he'd left you . . .'

'He would never leave me!'

'Oh, for Godsake! I didn't come here to talk about *him*.'

'I'll bet you didn't!'

Immediately he felt sorry for her, alone in this place, forced to wait and wait.

She had opened the door to him, and he might have come to betray her or strangle her, for all she knew. She was as helpless as any soldier.

'Are you really only nineteen?' he asked her.

'I'm twenty. I should be twenty-one next January.'

Next January. Next winter. It was unreal; he could not imagine her in another winter.

'Rosaleen, I'm going away.'

'Don't say my name!'

'I'm leaving Ireland. Come with me.'

'Aren't you forgetting something?'

'Do you want your baby to grow up here?'

'Oh, so the child's included in the invitation!'

He felt defeated by her tiredness, by the room, by the baby. 'I have to go, Rosaleen. But I can't go without you.'

'Listen, what happened between us is to do with this place. Oh, OK, you made me feel alive. I love . . . I thank you . . . for that.'

'You prefer to feel dead.'

'You know what I'm scared of? That I'd be the same somewhere else . . .'

'I want you to be the same!'

She gave a reluctant smile.

'Do you believe in God?' he asked.

'No.'

He was disappointed. 'Don't you pray, then?'

'All the time.'

He began to smile as he watched her, the way her face frowned and cleared again, the way her rings reflected the firelight.

189

'Please,' she said very softly, 'don't do that.'

She didn't look like a mother. Didn't smell like one either.

Suddenly they were kissing. She moaned and let go of him.

'We must hurry,' he whispered.

'Yes, yes,' she shook her head dreamily.

'It's time to go.'

'Why are they sending you away?'

He reddened. 'I'm going absent without leave.'

'Oh no! Gerry!'

'Don't worry. So far it's legit. I have an off-duty pass. I've a hired car parked outside a private house. I'm going to drive to Dublin taking an unmarked road over the border and then I'll dump the car. Fly somewhere in Europe.'

'Oh God, listen to the globetrotter! You have to figure out a way to get to the end of this street first. You're not the Invisible bloody Man!'

He grinned. 'You see, you do care for me.'

'Marriage is indissoluble.'

'Only second marriages,' he teased her.

She made an almost imperceptible movement towards him. 'Gerry, aren't you terrified they'll catch you?'

'No. I'm not afraid of anyone now. For the first time in my life.'

He sounded like Clint Eastwood. The sentiment was as ill-fitting as the suit. 'That's not true,' he said. 'I'm afraid of being caught. I'm also afraid of not being caught, but I don't expect you to understand that!'

'I do. It's easy to be a slave ... You know what I decided yesterday?'

He could not answer. He was mortified. She thought he was a slave.

'The only people I respect are the ones who despise the law. People who make their own rules ...' Suddenly, her voice broke. 'Gerry, I think about death all the time. It drives me insane.'

She rushed to be held by him.

'Leave here, I'll give you plenty of other things to think about.'

But she broke away again and went over near the cot. 'You don't understand what it's like to have a child. Even if I left him ... if I *could* leave him ... I'd never be free of the thought of him.'

'Bring him. I told you!'

'Oh, you know we can't go with you. You're on the run. It's

190

dangerous, it's uncertain. I can't risk my son! Besides, I don't have exclusive rights over him, remember.'

Everything she said depressed Gerry, because he knew she was right.

'What will you do then? Go on rotting alive in this dump. Obviously I can't leave you alone here. I wouldn't know what was happening . . . I've got to go back to the barracks.'

She ran out of the room. He was still wondering what to do when she returned, carrying wads of used banknotes. 'Gerry, here. Take it.'

'Where the hell did you get all this?'

'It's too long a story. Just take it, will you? It'll help you until you find work.'

'You're trying to buy me off.'

She laughed nervously. 'I can't worry over two of you, can I?'

'Why not?' he thought. For a moment he hated her. She was someone's wife, after all. Never. The idea slipped into him and sank deep.

Never.

He would never. She would never.

His escape was pointless now, without glamour. He saw himself in a strange country. He would be a foreigner, someone in the background, using up the years. She would forget him. She wanted to forget him.

'You have to care for both of us,' he answered.

She closed her eyes quickly. She was trembling, spreading her hands.

A sober happiness filled him. 'I've hurt you. You do love me,' he thought.

He kissed her into calmness, long experimental kisses without the headlong suddenness of before. He felt safe in the windowless room, free of the sense of vulnerability in his neck and back which he had suffered for months. He dropped to his knees and raised her night-dress, covering her thighs with kisses and then gently pressing his mouth to her vulva. Gradually her body unclenched and she caressed his hair. He felt his chest contract with the strange anguish of love, which no amount of love-making could lighten. He had to leave her to that man who had the right to embrace her innumerable times, her lawful husband, the father of her child. Their child . . .

191

She kneeled beside him and kissed the marine aftertaste of herself on his mouth. She spoke suddenly: 'You're crying!'

It was good to cry. He had not cried enough. Terrible to be always with men, unable to cry.

They clung together for a while until at last he had to go if he was to get beyond the patrol-infested area and clear the border in time.

'God bless you,' were her last words to him. He said nothing.

He stepped out into the dark Irish night. 'This must be reality,' he thought.

He moved fast and cautiously, a pain in his throat. The whole city seemed to be crouching in fear. 'Is it my fear?' he wondered, caressing the revolver through his jacket. 'You don't have to go, don't have to . . .' His feet fled forward, and then the car wheels were rushing him through the terrible bloody North of Ireland. Every mile was like a piece torn from his life.

'Why am I running away from you, Rosaleen?'

'Never,' he thought. 'Never.'

## 22

Her hair was lank and her face looked grey.

'We're like everybody else now,' he thought.

'You haven't slept either,' he said.

'I couldn't . . . not knowing if you were safe . . .'

'I was safe all right. In safe hands.'

He did not want her to touch him. His bones ached. He suspected his breath must be foul.

'Did they abuse you, Dan?'

'When did they . . . inform you? That I was detained?'

'They didn't! I only found out yesterday. By chance.'

'Bastards!'

They were both suddenly looking at a heap of fivers scattered on the rug before the fire. He felt his face turn red with shame. 'Blood will out,' a voice said in his mind.

'Where did you get it? Won't you tell me, Dan?'

'Rosaleen, please, I've had enough questions!'

As he sat down, his hand discovered the bottle of brandy and glass left forgotten beside the chair since the night, the last night he had been home. He poured himself a glass.

'Must celebrate. My regained freedom!'

She turned away in distress.

'What is it?' he asked.

'It's the way you held the bottle with such tenderness! Dan, please don't drink.'

He sipped the brandy, although her reproof ruined the taste.

She spoke gently to him: 'You see, you want to destroy yourself. I don't know why, but you do! Drink is one way. Debts are another. Whatever made you interesting to the army for three days, that's another! I don't want to be part of your defeat!'

She sounded so sincere and desperate, he could not resent her. 'My drinking is no different from your drugs, Rosaleen. That's the

193

worst thing about marriage — no private degradation!. . . I want a bath.'

'Wait, Dan!. . . Oh, why do you always walk away?'

'Because I can't run!'

'A right comedian you are!'

Ascending the stairs hurt his stomach, but he did not care. He was longing to soak in the bath, to lie there and wallow for as long as he liked.

The bathtub was full of steeping laundry! Dan burst into tears. Rosaleen appeared.

'What is it?'

'That's what he called me as well!'

'Who?'

'You did.'

'I haven't done anything!'

'A comedian. That's what you all think.'

She tried to hold him, making him flinch. Seeing her hurt look, he raised his sweater quickly to reveal the bruises. They were both crying now.

'I couldn't go on living . . .' she wept.

'I don't want to destroy myself,' he said. 'Someone saved my life. Spared my life.'

'Brendan McCartney?'

'Yes.'

'What happened?'

'Killed himself. Didn't kill me. Luck of the draw!' he laughed nervously.

'But why, Dan? Won't you tell me?'

'He thought he had the right . . . I'm tired,' he said, turning to look at the bath. Rosaleen moved forward to pull out the plug, and started wringing the bundles of laundry and throwing them into a bowl on the floor. He pulled off his stale clothes while she filled the bath with hot water and sweet-smelling stuff.

'Some food would be nice,' he said, wanting to get rid of her. But when he was immersed in the water, he realized that he was sore with hunger. He began to rush, stinging himself with the soap as he washed off the caked blood. He wanted bread and butter, eggs, jam, and tea. His hunger ruled out every other thought. He flung on the robe that was hanging on the back of the door and went downstairs again. Rosaleen was slumped in a chair. She looked dully at him.

'There's no food in the house.'

'What? Nothing?'

'Let's leave here! We've got to get out!'

'No. No.'

'Why on earth . . .? You're dreaming, Dan. You're compromised. You have no choice.'

'Look, I know Brendan was wrong. But I have to reply to him. I have to give him an honourable reply.'

'How will you do that? Hold a séance? Brendan is dead! . . . Do we have to be ruled by the dead?'

'He had courage and I want to have courage. To live my own way. To refuse to be coerced.'

'Courage is a lack of imagination! Oh, Dan, please don't risk everything for your latest image of yourself!. . . You were the one who said we can't quarrel with guns.'

'We must quarrel with guns.'

She was silent for a few moments.

'Where do I fit into this picture?' she asked finally.

'What?'

'While you're out there making your stand, dodging the Provos, what shall I do?'

'What do you mean?'

She stooped to the floor and began to gather up the money in handfuls, smoothing out the folded notes and stacking them in her lap.

'We can't all be heroes, you know! Most people live here by going dead inside. By taking up drink or sports . . . Maybe I should join that big army of tracksuits?' She spilled some of the money and let it lie.

'You're better than most people,' he said.

She looked appalled. 'I tried to give away this money,' she spoke quietly. 'To a soldier. A deserter.'

'What!'

'He came to the house.'

'To *this* house?'

'You should never have left me alone!' she said wildly.

'But why? Why did he come here?'

'I wasn't myself . . . I haven't been myself for ages . . .'

It dawned on him what had happened with a brutal visual clarity.

A swaggering Brit laying her bare, entering her . . .

'No, I don't believe it! You didn't . . .'

'Oh, don't! Please forgive me . . .'

'Was it in our bed?' he wondered.

He felt his hand double into a fist. 'Did you tell *him* he wouldn't be stealing anything from me?'

'You'll never understand!' she said.

'I suppose you "love" him?' he spoke nastily.

'Oh Christ, it had nothing to do with loving him! It was to do with hating everything else!'

'Me?'

She was silent. They remained in opposite corners of the room, unable to bear each other, unable to leave.

He knew it was only because he looked so beaten that she dared tell him such a thing. He looked like the sort of husband . . . the sort of man . . . the sort of non-man . . . What a joke! While he had been up to his neck in lies and dangers and squalor, she was . . . So was she! 'You are me, you bitch,' he thought.

What an idiot he had been to think he could start afresh! The squalid money was lying on the floor. Rosaleen had . . . Betrayal, he thought. Infidelity. My wife has betrayed me. He felt nothing. But then the vision of the act itself caught him. Bodies hurling themselves at each other, words, exclamations, bedsprings. His head was aching.

Ridiculous to imagine he could have a better life.

Suddenly he remembered Mrs Dwyer. No, he decided. No, I won't give in. He looked at Rosaleen out of the corner of his eye. How unhappy she was! You have to be alive to feel pain, he thought.

He stood. 'I'm going to get some food.'

'We could sell the house.'

'Why?'

'Everything's ruined. You think I don't love you.'

Everything is not ruined, he thought. I'm alive. She's alive. He walked forward and stood beside her. She was to the right of him, not looking, breathing fast.

'Which half of the baby would you prefer?' he said at last.

All Futura Books are available at your bookshop or newsagent, or can be ordered from the following address:
Futura Books, Cash Sales Department.
P.O. Box 11, Falmouth, Cornwall.

Please send cheque or postal order (no currency), and allow 55p for postage and packing for the first book plus 22p for the second book and 14p for each additional book ordered up to a maximum charge of £1.75 in U.K.

Customers in Eire and B.F.P.O. please allow 55p for the first book, 22p for the second book plus 14p per copy for the next 7 books, thereafter 8p per book.

Overseas customers please allow £1 for postage and packing for the first book and 25p per copy for each additional book.